The *Apple* You Were Fed

Mill City Press, Inc.
212 3rd Avenue North, Suite 570
Minneapolis, MN 55401
1.888.MILLCITY
www.millcitypress.net

ISBN 13: 978-1-934248-74-4
ISBN 10: 1-934248-74-6
LCCN: 2007941982

Cover design by James Wilkinson / Dzyn Lab
Interior set in Adobe Garamond Pro by Dzyn Lab

Printed in the United States of America

Some of the names in this book have been changed.

Kimberly Lisowski   Andrea Pouliot

The *Apple* You Were Fed

MILLCITY
PRESS

Dedication

To

Eliana, Isaiah, & Tirzah
And
Katelyn, Kennedy, David, & Karaline

Table of Contents

Preface

Our scheduled lives of method and routine afford us the comfort of efficiency, or maybe, the lack of certain disruptions. We like knowing what comes next. We take the same routes to and from the same places we consistently go and can guess the endings of the movies we watch. Books almost always follow familiar guidelines too, having well-defined styles. Readers always know what to expect, and while lessons are possibly learned, it is this repeating predictability that lulls us into the patterns robbing our lives of life. In essence, whether we're in a jet fighter or a crop duster, we're on auto pilot. Jesus would say we are sleeping.

One of the first signs of this slumber-induced existence is the irritation felt when life doesn't seem to be as we had anticipated. So please postpone expectation in order to be roused from *your* sleep, so you can take the controls and fly the way originally intended. This book has entertaining elements usually reserved for a story but also conveys information in much the same way a doctor might make clear a diagnosis, straightforwardly and with purpose. Our hope is to communicate, through deeply personal and open writing, the progression we took and the truth we found. What we seek to share is not the memoir, but the message, which is encapsulated in a book but could be shared a million other ways. You are invited to be an audience, a participant, a critic, and awake.

ection 1

Shedding the Skin

Chapter 1

Authenticity:
I'm Never Eating Soup Again

We see people everyday in schools, grocery stores, and on street corners. They are everywhere. Some we avoid; others we feel drawn to meet, and on very rare occasions, we meet someone with whom we actually connect. Without question, the people in our lives create the pleasure and the pain. But sometimes when least expected, when we don't realize our need and seemingly by chance, we bump into someone who shapes the course of our destiny, somebody who helps us unearth the lie of our lives.

Kimberly
The paper on the exam table crinkled under me as I shifted uncomfortably in front of the doctor. My arm reached involuntarily to take the prescription he offered,

the one that would make me "feel better." I watched the doctor's mouth moving and thought how odd it seemed that he looked like he was underwater; I realized, for the first time in as long as I could remember, my eyes had welled with tears. *Can't you hear me? I'm not depressed!* It was my third visit to yet another doctor, with the same results. I folded the paper together with the others in my purse and went back to convincing myself I could keep it all together.

I thought I had created a pretty nice existence for myself, but as the autumn leaves yellowed and ignited into varying crimson hues, my life began to feel as barren as the trees were certain to become. Surveying all I'd acquired in 11 years of marriage, I didn't know whose stuff I was looking at. I did not recognize my own reflection in the mirror, the stuff I'd purchased, or even the job I had. There was no real joy in any of it. In fact, it felt pointless. My agnostic tendencies left me trying to rely upon the old books and theories that helped me earn my BA in Psychology, but I was held captive by an internal struggle. My mind would not let up on the question, *What is the point to this life?*

On Halloween night it all came bubbling out. The cool windy air foretold of an evening storm, both in the skies and within me. Dark thoughts taunted while I tried to pass out candy to the neighborhood kids, *People are starving and you're giving candy to children who have everything...* My head felt dizzy; my emotions churned with the whipping wind, *What is the point to this life?* The buildup had been coming for weeks... months, maybe even years and was now erupting to the surface. This time, it was out of my control.

Ed will be back with the kids soon, I chanted to myself, trying to settle down. As the rain began to pour, I stepped off the porch into the storm. I was going to out run my turmoil or chase it down; I was running for my life. I ran until too exhausted to go any farther. Slipping in the mud, I slumped to the ground, where everything inside my soul emptied out into the night. The running, the screaming, the sweating; it poured out with the rain.

"Why is this happening to me?" I shouted. Slowly rocking, I hugged my knees to my chest crying for the times I held in my emotions. Crying over the decisions I'd made, decisions that changed me, I wept for everything I'd lost in myself and for the torture it would take to reclaim it all.

The gray clouds parted slightly to reveal the full moon, shedding barely enough light to let me know I was in an unfamiliar place. As the storm settled, I gathered myself to start the long walk home. Smoothing my wet hair behind my ear, I employed a flawed but trusted strategy; pick yourself up when you are down. *I have to be ok for my family,* I cautioned.

Trying to explain the wet clothes to my husband, Ed, later that night; I concealed most of the personal details in my usual way. Emotions always felt too dramatic or too exaggerated for the reasons behind them. Who cared about some silly little story I would tell or the boring details of life that were too insignificant to waste time discussing? Trying to relate, he did his best to listen, but it never seemed enough. I needed so much, too much.

Andrea

On twenty acres at the edge of a very small town, I was oblivious to any pattern in the seemingly random way people came into and went out of my life. I usually blamed differences of opinion or lifestyle or bad timing for the fact that I was lonely. I blamed my husband, Tony, and I blamed the broken church we'd been forced out of, but never, ever did it occur to me that I could have some fault in the way things had worked out. I prayed for real friendships and studied my *Bible*. I read books and wrote in prayer journals, kind of sinking in the mire with the Word of God in my hands.

My children attended a private Christian school, and apart from dropping them off and picking them up, weeks would pass when I didn't have a reason to leave our house. I tried to use my time wisely, and when feelings of despair threatened, I begged myself to be content. Sitting in the window seat, staring out at the empty road, condemnation would wear on me as I struggled to understand why I just couldn't learn to love the nice life I had been blessed with. I had a handsome, devoted husband, three gorgeous, well behaved children, and a great house. I couldn't figure out why I felt so drained.

When the tired monotony of our world was interrupted by Tony's idea to move into a neighborhood an hour away, where the kids would go to public school, I was as excited as I was afraid. I wondered what God thought of our plan, so I spent hours seeking some indication that we were making the right decision. Even without reassurance, before we ever put our house up for sale, I was making packing reports and moving check lists on the computer. I safely tucked away my hope for something better.

Kimberly

At the beginning of that long winter, Ed and I decided to build a new house, in a new town. Changing our address always kept us preoccupied; this would be our fourth move in nine years. We looked at new developments around the upscale little community of Canfield, Ohio, where we found Westbury Park.

Over the months of planning and building, I had pulled myself together, but I had been to the bottom and felt the despair; it was still looming there, a looming threat. I kept one eye focused on suppressing those feelings and the other turned away to avoid them. Of course, on the outside, I maintained my witty sense-of-humor and shiny hair. No one would have suspected my ongoing silent struggle for meaning. I'd read how a deer will instinctively move toward water out in the wild. Somehow, they understand their panting is not just out of thirst but out of a deeper need, one that tells them they can't survive without it. I intuitively sought the water of life, too. I had no idea I was about to move across the street from a woman hungering in the same way, a woman who would share in this search with me.

Andrea

Driving through Westbury Park, I could tell it was designed to be a warm and charming development, accented with tree lined roadways and period lamp posts flickering yellow by sundown. The matching signposts and mailboxes appealed to my need for order and congruence.

Although my husband had chosen the community and the neighborhood, his anxieties about living so near to other families rivaled my own. We didn't want anyone imposing upon our free time, and we didn't want a house full of screaming neighbor kids. He made sure to go over the rules of maintaining our distance from people every time we drove out to see what the builders had accomplished. As much as I wanted to help protect our privacy, first impressions of the new neighbors kept me as interested as the details of the construction. We saw a couple about the same age as us anxiously checking progress on the house they were building directly across the street. Trying to count their children, I made sure to wave to them from my seat on the damp wooden ramp serving as the makeshift stairs into our partially built house. I wanted them to think we were nice, but we drove home wondering if all four of the children with them were theirs. After several occasions of smiling from a distance through weeks of building, we eventually met Kimberly and Ed and discovered their home was scheduled to be completed at the same time as ours.

Kimberly

With my busy schedule, packing began weeks in advance. I found myself retrieving boxes from the attic unopened from previous moves. One box stuck out in particular as it was marked, "baby stuff." The youngest of my four *babies* was now almost three years old, so I thought about just tossing it out without looking inside. Curiosity won out, and peeling back the yellowed tape from the cardboard, I was surprised at the contents. Like a time capsule, it held tiny little Christmas dresses and infant toys I must have packed up from the starter home Ed and I lived in when we were newly married. Our first two babies were girls, and I had kept the items just in case we would ever need them again, but they ended up lost in the shuffle of three successive moves.

I held up a little red satin dress four month old Kennedy wore for her first Christmas. Katelyn, just three at the time, had a pair of patent leather shoes in the box. I folded the dress and set some of the other items beside me then flung the mostly empty box onto the floor below.

A clanking sound echoed through the garage. I looked down to see a shiny Christmas ornament beaming in the sunlight. Climbing down from the attic, I recognized it immediately. It was engraved, "Edward and Kimberly." *I thought I'd lost this*, I said to myself.

It was a reminder of the huge Christmas Eve fight that almost ended our marriage. I was sure it would be my last holiday as a married woman. At the time, I saved the ornament because it allowed me to remember that Ed and I did love each other; I wanted to keep it. It was ironic, opening that box, because we managed to pull ourselves together enough to last another seven years. Now we were moving again. For a moment, I felt sick to my stomach, realizing a pattern I was locked into yet couldn't escape. I felt the familiar anxiety start to bubble, but I squashed it down with one colossal mind sweep. *I have always made it. I'll be fine.*

Andrea

Kimberly and Ed seemed like the perfect couple. They were a little too relaxed and comfortable though, because they invited us over the first weekend we both moved into our homes despite the messy chaos of disheveled rooms not fully unpacked. We reluctantly accepted and walked across the street with our appropriate nice-to-meet-you demeanors. Holding hands, Tony and I tried to avoid stepping in dirt on the wet street, while he reminded me not to be an "open book" in the new neighborhood. We were going to be good, Christian, Republican neighbors whose kids would never bother anyone. To avoid pushy people who could potentially become too friendly, he wondered aloud if he'd have to retrieve our mail under the cover of darkness. I reminded him whose decision it was to move us to a neighborhood. We were trying, but living in a development was such a change from our previous home; a change which in some ways, offered us a chance to start over without the mistakes of the past.

Ed led us on a tour of their stately brick colonial. It had a Tuscan villa feel on the inside with bistro signs and candles and the undeniable elements of Feng Shui. Breathing in the scent of their home, I noticed how it matched the colors -- warm vanilla and creamy coffee, mingling with sweet caramel. There was not a corner, a ledge, or a piece of wall that wasn't decorated in full display, from the beaded silk purse draped with dainty whimsy over the arm of her sofa to the reaching stems of grandly portioned floral arrangements. It was beautiful; I was impressed.

Enjoying their company and happy to see our kids having fun playing together, I invited them to see our house right then, too. Tony turned and directed a telling glare at me, as I blew our agreed upon façade. I pressed into the familiar awkwardness of trying to be myself without upsetting my husband, hoping he would understand I was caught up in the thrill of the moment.

Kimberly

Tony and Andrea seemed friendly, yet a bit stuffy, like church people but with cuter clothes. We agreed to go tour their home, secretly grinning to each other knowing we'd already sneaked in a few times during the months of building. Ed put his arm around me squeezing as we walked. He was so excited to be making new friends. His idea of a neighborhood was one filled with driveway bar-b-ques and multitudes of kids tossing balls and riding bikes. Wanting to fill our weekends with fun plans, I knew

Ed was glad we were meeting another new family in the neighborhood.

Their home was done in a traditional style, and even though boxes were still lying around the rooms, the house felt warm and elegant like a softly lined wool coat. Andrea's kitchen was somewhat artistic as it had all the makings of intense planning and design, telling me someone in the family knew how to cook. Tony walked us room by room, each painted in different but complementary colors of light beiges, orange reds, and chocolate browns. Pointing out the sitting room off the master bedroom, Andrea said, "This is where I'll do my *Bible* study."

Bible study! No, no, no, don't ruin the potential friendship just yet, "Oh good," I replied without forethought trying to be accommodating. Ed shot me a look documenting my unfamiliar façade, but I pushed through the awkwardness with a joke, "I could use some of that!"

Laughing about having too many kids and not enough money left to furnish our new homes felt like a stand up show. Bantering and the clever sort of comments usually reserved for more well known company flowed effortlessly between us, and my side ached from laughing as we bounced from story to story. Leaving, we thanked them for such an enjoyable beginning in our new neighborhood.

Reminiscing later at home, I unfolded the new down comforter onto our four-post, cherry bed. "I must admit," I said to Ed, as he lit my favorite sandalwood candle, "I really had fun tonight, but I'm a bit skeptical about what to talk about beyond our kids and these houses. After all, Andrea has a *Bible* room, a whole room just for religion!"

Laughing, Ed teased, "You ...skeptical? You're the one who said you couldn't wait to study the *Bible* with her!" He was trying to ease my mind, knowing religion and religious people had always posed a problem for me. As a child, I spent years attending church yet spent most of the time wishing I were still at home in bed. I could never relate to the smiley people either with their lack of emphasis on fun or even fashion for that matter. Church resembled a big masquerade. No one in the real world acted that way.

Sitting down on the bed he added, "I feel the same way, but we can't write someone off just because they're ultra religious. They seemed normal to me." We did have that rare couple chemistry where the men enjoyed each other's company as much as the women did, so I ignored my skepticism deciding to extend an invite for coffee the next day after the kids filed on the bus for school.

Andrea

Within weeks any fear I had of an intrusive friendship dissolved into a welcomed morning routine: the bus stop, sweeping floors, loading dishes, and waiting for a call from Kimberly. I would run through my house making beds and dusting while my kids dressed themselves so I could have most of my work finished in time for our morning phone call, which often evolved into visits with pots of coffee and hot buttery biscuits.

Making time for each other as often as we could, we found we both enjoyed debating and discussing contemporary issues. Though rarely in agreement, we loved hearing each other's perspectives. Kimberly expressed herself in a way that stimulated conversation without provoking defensiveness, and as long as the topics were political or social, or when we talked about our children, it was effortless. She could talk about every controversial or pop culture topic, but if asked to share her emotions, she would turn blotchy and red, reverting to a blubbering junior high school girl. I was good at avoiding those areas of discussion, and since she was much more at ease when I was talking, I began telling her all about myself.

I was amused listening to ~~Andrea's~~ *Kimberly* take on life, liberty, and the pursuit of happiness. We were addicted, just as much to the female companionship as to the java. Confident in my ability to not judge anyone, I had the gift of parents and grandparents who always taught me racism and prejudice were ugly character traits. Yet, the thought occurred to me after those first few weeks with my new Christian friend, I *was* judgmental. I was intolerant to Christians. Too often, at their worst, I found them hypocritical and even arrogant; and at their best, naïve and out-of-touch. However, generalizing people and grouping them together as a single unit had cast me into the very cess pool of hypocrisy I claimed to despise. The first lesson learned in my friendship with Andrea was how easily prejudice can be masked by denial and a lack of examination of a well touted personal belief system. I was shocked at my oversight. It was wrong.

Thinking over all my previous friendships, I considered, one by one, the tired patterns and eventual distance suffered in each of them. How we, as women, have a tendency to hurt one another through gossip and jealousy or consistently put everyone else above ourselves until there is nothing left of our own lives we recognize. I wanted to stop the cycle. Deciding to discuss it with her personally, I challenged myself to have the guts to be vulnerable.

As the morning sun lit her stainless steel appliances, I sat at the kitchen counter in shock watching Andrea rinse a headless chicken and put it into a pot on the stove. Gesturing to the gutted bird floating in the water, I said, "I'm never eating soup again." The smell of peppered water soon turned to warm broth and tempted my decision, but who was I kidding? My idea of cooking was frozen pizza and raw cookie dough.

After the first few minutes, the conversation deepened. Nervous but resolved I felt myself searching for the perfect wording. *I have no idea what I'm doing, but here I go.* Sensing the seriousness, Andrea instinctively leaned in and rested her elbows on the counter as I asked, "Do you realize we have a perfect chance to start this friendship in a totally honest and authentic way?" I maintained eye contact and continued, "What if we drop pretenses, and are real? If we think or feel something we should say it -- no pretending to be fine if we're not." I felt myself flushing and ignored the heat rushing to my face. Andrea stared back expressionless while I went on, "For example, we'll give each other the freedom to say if something bothers or hurts one of us, and we shouldn't try to impress each other. We should just accept we are both women trying to do the best we can... a *real* friendship, with no pretense, no judgment, no games." It felt like a promise, one I was making and one I was asking Andrea to make.

Andrea

I acted as if Kimberly's idea sounded great. It did in some ways; great but impossible. Every aspect of what she was suggesting plowed through me. It pierced an issue at the heart of how I showed the world who I was. I was polite. Wondering if I could be completely honest *and* polite, I realized authenticity would require me to say *no*, which I'd never been able to do. I was also certain I would struggle saying if something she did bothered or hurt me. I would be far more at ease absorbing the offense than addressing it. I could talk about anything, even embarrassing personal things, but telling another person when I felt troubled by her seemed confrontational. I could hear the blood rushing past my ears as I gave Kimberly permission to blow by the carefully constructed barriers Tony and I used to stay in control of our privacy.

I knew Kimberly had a degree in psychology, and for a second, I felt accused of being disingenuous. I had always intensely hated psychology and had a great deal of reasons why I thought it to be evil and foolish. In my mind, psychology was the science of blame shifting. I had no patience for the nonsense of pointing my finger at my parents and their parents and then being blamed for the things my kids did or didn't do. It was all ridiculous to me. I sensed no judgment from Kimberly, though, because she seemed to be enthusiastically optimistic about our chances of surviving the pitfalls of gossip, hurt feelings, and misunderstandings. It felt as if she had stepped out from behind her degree and was asking me to step out from behind what made me feel secure. Unsure of how to live outside the fortress of my life but ready for something different; I agreed to what she was asking.

Kimberly

Stepping out of our comfort zones was not going to be easy, especially for me. I began questioning my suggestion immediately, because I knew myself. I had never been open or vulnerable to anyone, even as a child. I was a strong career woman who could handle anything. My feelings were a non-issue because they were a sign of weakness, so I showed the world my controlled, pulled-together, successful side at all times. *Why did I just promise to unveil the side of me in torment over who I was, what I was... who I wanted to become?*

Chapter 2

Dreams:

What Part of Me is Gone?

Andrea

As the next few days passed, I thought about my previous prayers for real friendship. I was happy with my new social life and aware of the surface we were beginning to break, so I tested the waters of genuineness almost immediately. I worried about being analyzed by the psychology person, but I pushed past the fear. In a moment of complete abandon, I began telling Kimberly about a dream that had me upset. I prefaced my telling of the nightmare with a **disclaimer** acknowledging how irritating it was when adults talked about their dreams.

I barely uttered the first words, "I dreamt I murdered a..." when Kimberly interrupted me asking for a piece of paper. Picking up a pen from the counter, she scribbled what appeared to be a grocery list. I leaned closer, nonchalantly trying to see what it said, but when finished, she flipped it over.

Resting her hand on the paper with a delicate pat indicating for me to go on talking, Kimberly said, "I'm sorry, what were you saying?"

Tempted to tell her to forget it, I wondered, *Why am I doing this,* but continued, "I murdered her, a girl -- the girl in my dream. I was trying to figure out what was happening, why it was happening. The rain was coming down; my heart was racing, and I tried to see her face. I couldn't tell who she was, but I had killed her; that was certain. The wind kept gusting, blowing. The huge layers of her white dress billowed up and then rested; I thought she was moving. The satin and tulle were soaked in blood. I couldn't think past the first sight of her lifeless body, a body I had to bury. My muscles were still and then trembling, the way your body shakes from the core out when you're in labor or freezing cold."

Pausing, I stood barefoot on the hardwood floor acting out the kind of shaking I meant. Kimberly didn't even smile when I emphasized with sound effects. I went on, "I don't know where I found a shovel. I just started digging. I was crying and shaking and heaving huge loads of dirt out of the ground. Rain pooled in the hole making it harder to dig. My arms were burning, but I kept digging until I was numb. I must have dragged her, rolling her into the grave; I don't know. It was raining; her blood was all over me. I didn't see her face. I couldn't see who she was, but the muddy dirt landed over her. My clothes and hair were soaked with blood and mud and rain. Throwing down the shovel and dropping to the ground, I shoved and pushed the mud into the hole."

Kimberly sat motionless with her hand still resting on the paper. Her eyes were fixed on me as she remained forward on the stool with a hollow expression. Conscious of how exposed I felt, I continued, "Peeling off my clothes, I stood in the shower, reeling from the horror of what had just happened. I feared opening my eyes, afraid of a dead girl, thinking she would be standing there. I scrubbed it all off, scratching and lathering and rinsing until there was no more hot water. I murdered a girl, and I had no idea why."

Taking a sip of coffee, I considered stopping there, but with no response from Kimberly, I broke the silence saying, "After killing her, I lived under a cloud of fear, shame, and confusion. I raised my kids; I was a good wife. It was a blur, but I managed to proceed through it, day by day. My family never knew.

When my youngest daughter was away at school, when I was older but not old, the police came. 'The gig is up,' they yelled into a bullhorn. The lights flashed and I heard a siren burst with sound. Before I knew what to do, my husband was standing at the door, reaching to open it.

My thoughts moved in slow motion, and the knot in my stomach tightened. Looking at the door, hearing the voices, I saw my husband's face. He was confused, unaware of what was about to happen, what I had done and how I would pay for it. He opened the door. An unbelievable hysteria flooded over me. *Do something. Somebody do something!*

As the officer pushed my head down guiding me, handcuffed, into the cruiser, I closed my eyes. I was going to be spending the rest of my life alone, separated from my husband and my children. I was going to prison. Then,

I woke up sweating, shaking, and realized it was just a dream."

I stood in front of Kimberly whose eyebrows were raised in awe; her mouth was slightly open as if a silent "oh" had escaped with her breath. I was split between great relief and horror wondering if her astonishment was due to the nature of my dream or the dramatic and over detailed way I told every part of it.

She flipped over the paper, but before I could see what it said, she picked it up, clutching it tightly in her fist. Her eyes darted around the kitchen before coming to rest on the words she'd written. Hesitating, she lowered it back to the counter and slid it toward me. As I read what she had written, my mind spun into total confusion. Scrawled across the crumpled paper was a series of bullet points:

- Murdered a young girl — buried her body
- Don't know who/how
- Lived in fear
- Kids grow up – cops come, "Gig is up, we know it was you"
- Horrified at being separated from Ed and my kids

"What is this?" I asked, knocking a knuckle on the paper, "I don't understand."

"That is *my* dream from two nights ago," her voice was barely a whisper.

I laughed, mostly because I didn't know what else to do. I looked at the paper in front of me disbelieving what I saw. Like a magic trick, it had to have an explanation.

Kimberly

Before Andrea told me her dream, I sensed what she was going to say. *I knew it!* She had said just a few words, but I had to stop her and write it down. Something told me to stop her. It was an impulse, a flicker. I could have just sat there and listened, but she wouldn't have believed me; I knew what she was going to say. That was my dream, my nightmare. I woke up feeling relieved it was just a dream but shaken over murdering someone and not knowing who or why. I grabbed the pen on impulse. I had to stop her and write it down. The usually noisy kitchen filled with our lively discussions went silent. For the first time, neither of us knew what to say.

I left right away, trying to gain some insight into our unusual morning. We didn't know how to react. It was a very odd and provocative experience, one that kept me awake for a few nights wondering why the perplexing details of the dream were strikingly identical. We both heard, "the gig is up," a phrase neither of us would say. How did we share that experience separately with such precision? It was not one of those go-to-school-on-test-day dreams that have one or two scenes and then ends. This dream had layers, emotions, characters, and grit. I thought about discussing Freud or Jung or dream analysis, but this seemed much too coincidental, deserving of more than a regurgitation of psych 101 from my college classes. Somehow, I became the client and analyzing myself was not that simple -- especially when the dream had more to do with the odd similarities than some outdated Freud cliché.

Andrea

We decided never to tell anyone and never to talk about it again; it was too weird. We didn't either, that is until I had a theory about what it meant. I was sitting on my front porch reading a book, which gave an account of a woman's growth and personal experience at mid-life. It explained how a woman can deny her true self, burying it deep within as she'd invested her life in living up to the expectations of others. Reading that made me wonder if the girl we had murdered in the dream could represent ourselves. It seemed possible to think I had wounded and could ultimately kill my true self, because I'd begun to notice how I rarely allowed myself to be vulnerable to others. It made me wonder if I were burying my wounded self beneath the Earth of forced smiles and *yes, we're doing fine-- please pass the salt,* type relationships.

I called Kimberly and awkwardly began asking her, "Do you think the dream shows the end result of what happens if we are not honest with ourselves? If we bury who we really are, acting out only part of ourselves, the part others want or expect -- is the outcome the loss of our intended lives…? Could that be the reason people freak out at mid-life? They realize the 'gig is up'. They realize they will never have anything real…" It wasn't the bold presentation of the theory I'd planned, it was more a string of questions than a statement.

Kimberly

Listening to Andrea talk of her theory, a barrage of thoughts littered my mind. *Was I the faceless dead girl in white?* This was not even a consideration until I realized the depth of that analogy. I certainly had a lot to conceal, a lot of baggage I carried. Contemplating how one day I would be forced to pay for that crime gave me a sudden perspective to my life never before seen. The price would be the loss of my authentic self. Buried under the assumptions or fears or even ignorance of the real me, I'd have lost years living out what I could have been. A life lost, physically and spiritually. *Was I the woman with no identity, gone forever...buried?* Although these thoughts were difficult to confront, I had to admit Andrea was right. *What part of me was gone?*

I did have a chain of events from my past that left me heart broken and changed, but I wasn't ready to discuss those details with Andrea just yet. In fact, I had never discussed them with anyone except Ed. I guess that meant I buried them. In psychology, the only thing to do would be to slowly uncover my past to explore why I had ended up in this position in life. The problem with that was how frightening it sounded and how much energy it would take to accomplish. I had no energy left most days with the job, kids, marriage. I had no time for more self-evaluation. The thought overwhelmed me, and having been through therapy before, it didn't resolve much long term anyway. This would have to come from within, more than a mind sweep; it would require brute effort to dig out the buried me with an authentic friendship as the catalyst.

Andrea

As Kimberly and I explored the idea of our dream being about our true selves, I thought about my life and how I had pretended to like things I disliked and agreed to ideas I didn't fully understand. I thought about the characteristic way I lived showing the world my diligent Christian housewife veneer. My life seemed to make sense biblically, but I could not deny the sometimes limited views I held of myself and others and how I allowed others to limit me. I even wondered if this boundary encircled my past friendships. Too few relationships seemed to weather the terrain of time. They almost all disintegrated, shattering under the burden of life and then blowing away with the winds of change. *Would that leave me with no identity, dead? Was there more to me than even I could recognize?* I too had to wonder, *What part of me was gone?*

My automatic reaction propelled me to my *Bible* but opening my concordance gave me a sense of stepping onto a treadmill. *I've done all of this before.* More *Bible* study felt like an exercise in getting back to nowhere. I was ready to explore in other directions to unearth some understanding about how much of me was buried. Reconfirming that there were verses about dreams, and that God spoke to people through dreams, wasn't going to rescue me from the awful results of burying myself. I needed to figure out what I was doing and why. The dream clearly showed it was *I* who killed and buried *myself.*

I began a systematic self-scrutiny which pierced the dirt piled atop my broken life allowing a single beam of light to penetrate the depths of where I really was spiritually and emotionally. The reality of what it would reveal was far removed from me, but Kimberly would prove to be the person instrumental in changing the course of my destiny. As I reflected over my life, I shared more than stories, I shared pieces of my decision-making history with her in hopes of finding that buried woman and deciphering what I must have missed in lessons I'd learned from the pulpit.

Kimberly

I had to have missed something from my professors, because I was waking up, rousing to the deep down knowledge of past mistakes and hungering to experience a better way. The dream forced us to recognize our lives and question our methods of living. It birthed a new way of relating, one in which we had no choice but to keep the promise, answering questions honestly, saying what we thought and openly listening while the other did the same. We were reaching beyond what we had always known in order to find something better. It took awareness to move away from what was familiar, an essential step in the process of learning from the other.

Answers more profound, life more fulfilling, façades blown away, these were the unstated goals of our lengthy talks. The dream opened up the undeniable need and desire to live out our true selves, no matter what it took or what had to be said. We could sense there was more to learn, something greater than we could have ever imagined. We had to go back and rewrite the dream, back to before the murder, to who we once were. *Was there a starting point?* Together, with verbal shovels and buckets of coffee, we began to uncover the buried women. The gig was up.

Chapter 3

Testimony:
Sitting on the Sidelines of Life

Andrea

I once heard a man with a funny accent say, "Life's a Johnny." My sister, Amy, and I made fun of him, laughing until we figured out what he meant. Journey, *Life's a journey.* The same as in life, his teaching was half over by the time we understood. I figured out my Johnny began on a Tuesday in May, the day my dad packed us up and boarded the Jesus train. Whether or not we started on the right track is an incidental notion in light of the fact that we ended up further from God than when we started. Trying to reach Him overshadowed my entire upbringing.

I know I had a childhood. I have pictures. I'm the girl off in the back, in the corner of the shot. My parents are in front. My dad is in the center; my mom standing proudly behind. There are Rich and Nate, my younger brothers, poking at each other, making faces. Amy is in the corner beside me. I'm in her shadow. We tried so hard. I can't say I recall being asked to step back, retreat. It was how it was from the moment I came into the world where two little girls believed they had a duty to quietly slip into the area carved out for them.

If the pictures were spilled into piles on the floor, there would be evidence of festive holiday meals and impromptu celebrations, gatherings of church people eating homemade spaghetti and fresh bread. There would be snap shots of me shaving my mother's floor length fur coat, and of gardens filled with vegetables and flowers. Sifting through the piles, one might see the six of us lying on my parent's bed talking or squeezing into the shower in our bathing suits. My exceptionally serious father would periodically emerge from his thoughts to wrestle on the floor under the heap of his four children, or to sing the chorus of his favorite church song while pounding the beat out with his fist. The pictures of us sitting in a circle sharing our kindest thoughts about each other in the candlelight wouldn't be untrue, but they would only be part of the story. They would be the side of us that made me want to protect our family and be loyal to it, to die for it if I had to.

As a submissive family, we allowed my father to decide what was important enough to address. He decided what things were shared with others and what things we spoke of in private, or not at all. Clearly-defined traditional roles were ingrained in our household, so I watched as my mother fought diligently every day to be the best she could at pleasing my father by cleaning and cooking and feeding my brothers a king's meal at their smallest whim.

Amy and I did our jobs as mini moms serving the men

and hoping they would approve, or at least not throw a fit if disapproving. We thought of them first while we busied ourselves in anticipation of their moods. My mother became obsessive, doing things like having no trash in the trash can. If one thing was thrown in, she stopped what she was doing, carried the garbage bag outside, and sprayed the can with disinfectant before putting in a clean bag. I had to become obsessive too, obsessively trying to find any way to not be noticed. *Be quiet; don't cause a problem.*

Once while eating an orange, I choked down every bit of skin and all of the seeds, but one. I couldn't swallow another thing. Looking around the kitchen, I thought of hiding the final seed in the mustard colored refrigerator, but I was afraid she would find it, the way she had found the pimentos from our chicken ala king in her change purse. I took a deep breath, resigning myself to the one reasonable alternative, my nostril.

The seed unfortunately migrated into my sinus cavity. My eyes watered, as the oblong nemesis spun and rolled with every breath. I gagged and coughed to no avail. I needed to be saved. We took the trip to the emergency room.

It wasn't what my mother would have wanted, and I didn't do it out of fear of what she would do to me if I made a mess. I was motivated by what a mess did to *her*. She was completely tortured by the destruction of her masterpiece, our home. If we stepped on the carpet, she dropped to her knees and rubbed out the footprints unless she had time to re-vacuum before my father came home. Our closets were color-coded and the linens pressed.

My mother was tall and beautiful, but she became thinner and thinner; something was clearly wrong with her. As her condition worsened during the following few years, Amy and I milled through our home as my mother mostly slept, sick in her bed. We became the moms then, taking care of my brothers and ourselves. Having lots of practice, it didn't even register to have a childhood of my own. Sunlight, motion, and noise made my mom sicker, so we had to be quiet and avoid causing problems. The condition of our house didn't matter when my mom thought she was dying. Nothing got done, but somehow, miraculously, we survived. Without sweeper lines or pressed linens, without a slippery wood floor shining in the foyer, we existed.

When she finally found medical help, a diagnosis of what she called endocrine melt down due to complications following Grave's disease, she opted not to go back to keeping a perfect house. Instead, with her new found energy, she left with my dad, night after night to go to church to serve God.

They never said *no* and people never stopped needing them; time, money, advice, whatever they had was for God to use. My dad gave away every other dollar he made to who ever needed help, while my mom opened our home for people to come to and even stay indefinitely if they needed to. Our family steadied the church and its people, yet we seemed to lack independent stability, as we moved from house to house trying to find the perfect life.

By the fifth grade, I had yet to consider my own needs above anyone else's. An invisible child has no needs or fears or expectations, and that was a set-up for a defining moment in my life. Hosting a weekly gathering, my parents fed and entertained their friends on Sundays following church. The women would visit and cook, while the men played football or volleyball in the back yard. Hours into the evening, we would all squeeze into the den off of our kitchen to eat and watch sports on TV.

On a colder Sunday, after eating chili with shredded cheese and sour cream, I was jolted from my quiet world by one of my father's friends. He was an especially tall and very confident man, who liked me enough to wrap his arms around me and whisper in my ear. I liked his big brother styled interest, so when he crawled behind me in the corner of our brown-plaid, sectional couch I bumped him with my elbow and returned my gaze to the game we were watching.

With a friendly looking glance in my father's direction, he pulled me back against himself, draped a blanket over us, and slipped his hand between my thighs. I gasped as he leaned in and breathed deeply through my hair and whispered, "It's ok." I wasn't ok, though. Blood was rushing to my face and other places too. My pulse was racing, and I didn't know what to do. Watching my mom walk across the room, for a moment, I felt myself reaching toward her to save me. With rough confidence, he told me that I should relax or I would embarrass my parents in front of everybody.

Pressed against him, I got my first lesson in what happens to a man when he touches a girl. Looking down at the blanket covering us and blinking back tears, I was paralyzed with fear. Playing out scenarios in my mind, I imagined myself standing up and thought somehow everyone would know. I never wanted anyone to know. Even aware of how wrong it was, I couldn't find a way to protest.

Much later, when I finally told my parents what had happened, they were shocked. Wincing as I spoke, my mother held her hand over her mouth. My dad's eyes, glazed with tears, were fixed to the floor; his wrinkled forehead and broken hearted frown told me a thousand things he couldn't bring himself to say. They never asked me any questions, though. "He touched me..." was all they wanted to know.

I couldn't fathom what a scene it would create when my dad confronted him or how embarrassing it would be for him once people knew he touched elementary school girls as an adult. Afraid I had let too much time pass, I wondered if it were too late to address what had happened. Apparently, my parents thought the same thing. They never said a word to anyone. My secret was safe with them. I guessed we had decided Jesus would want us to "forgive and forget." The message came through loud and clear, and I carried on the family tradition.

When my father was indicted by the federal government for a crime he did not commit, our world turned into chaos, but this time, everyone knew. He reported his employer after discovering the owners of the company were embezzling and laundering money, yet he was charged with them when indictments came down. Publicly, my parents maintained their optimism, but at home, they came undone. They went days without speaking and then breaking down in tears or yelling; my mom would be in a puddle, my dad in a rage.

They couldn't handle any extra pressure. Barely hanging on emotionally, they had stopped tuning in for the details about our lives. Our very presence in the room seemed to cause irritation. Even if we didn't ask for help or say we were hungry, my mom could tell we needed her and she was exasperated. Looking at us seemed to reminded her of a life she'd put on hold, a life that wasn't waiting patiently enough for her return.

During the four year investigation, my sister and I

were slipping through the cracks, figuring out the details of growing up, and learning quickly that everyone liked a girl afraid to say no. Together, our goal became living independently, almost thinking we could absorb some of the anxiety my parents felt into ourselves. We tried to make up for our two little brothers who took turns vying for attention; one trying to earn it through performance, the other demanding it with rage. There were many nights I cried myself to sleep from the intense fear of losing my dad and the strain of hiding how I felt about everything. Without my sister, life would have been unbearable. We encouraged each other, and our parents were proud of how resilient we were.

I was careful to never complain. I was also cautious of acting too upset when I had to change schools for the sixth time as we moved to my parent's hometown for emotional support. My parent's hometown... That's where we were drawn into a little non-denominational church pastored by my Uncle Will and Aunt Nora. They promised to help us if my dad went to prison. Nora had a way of convincing people she had a special gift, "the anointing," as she called it. She spoke using verses from the *Bible*, ending her bellowing commands with the words, "Thus sayeth the Lord." It gave the impression that God spoke through her. Hearing her promise deliverance from evil was the comfort my parents began to crave.

The evening before closing arguments were expected to be made, my father's attorney told him to pack a bag. He advised him not to anticipate returning home from court. Sitting on the landing at the top of our stairs, I listened as my parents debated who to believe -- the attorney, or "God." In the morning, I looked at my dad dressed in his blue suit, so handsome and stoic. There were a million mornings he went off to work dressed in those same important clothes, fixing companies with his brilliance, saving them from bankruptcy. No one was there to save him though, no one.

My mom sat in the car, staring through the windshield as my father took each of the four of us hugging and kissing us, declaring his love. Rich and Nate were so little, too young to cope with such a goodbye. My parents pulled out of the driveway, and the dust cloud behind them threatened to wipe away my father's last footsteps from our lives. We stood for a moment watching the car until it was almost out of sight; then gone. The four of us waited alone in the front yard huddled together shaking under the weight of pain. Amy and I fought back tears. My parents left the two of us in charge, so we gained control of our emotions. Back inside the house, I cleaned, while Amy prepared breakfast.

A sweet memory of my father swept through my mind as if it wanted to imprint onto my soul forever. As a young girl, he once used company letterhead to invite me to meet with him under the pool table in the basement after work. It was his way of making an ordinary event special and memorable. I remembered feeling the thrill of excitement and heading down early just to make sure I didn't miss anything. Waiting under the pool table, untwisting strands of the red carpet, I wondered what he was going to say. The steps quietly protested as he thumped toward the location of our secret meeting. Within seconds, he was on the floor crawling toward me with a ring box in his hand. Trying to concentrate on what he was saying, I couldn't stop myself from wondering what was in the box. When he was finished talking about being a Christian, he extended the gift out to me. Creaking as I opened it, the box held a beautiful gold cross on a thin gold chain. I loved it. I loved him.

Snapping free from the memory, I prayed to God to save him, "I'll glorify your name, if you could please, please save my dad, Lord..."

My brothers, sister, and I stood by the front window or in the kitchen by our phone. We fought, slept, cleaned, and watched television, anything to pass the hours. I heard a thud as Rich jumped down from his bed, yelling their car was coming up the driveway. Looking out the window, we watched in slow motion, seeing what resembled a cloth flag or scarf being waved in the passenger's side window. We all flew out the door to witness the emotional explosion. There, fidgeting for the door handle, face covered sobbing into the cloth, was my father. "I'm free!" We heard his muffled shouts through the closed window. "It's over! I'm free!" He'd been cleared of all the charges.

Having been freed from conviction, my parents entered deeper into a spiritual prison with a passion unparalleled. It didn't matter what happened as long as we were making the Word of God look good from the curb. We were all about smiling in front of people as a way of glorifying God, living as if true emotion would sully up our claims about Jesus. We died to "self," showing Christ to the world. My dad gave his time and money as if paying back what he thought he owed to God in gratuity, and my mother kept a festive home as a source of hospitality, although we continued whittling down who was included in our lives.

I struggled at first to keep my promise to glorify God for saving my dad. Being in high school, everything made me feel guilty, and church was somewhere I felt I didn't deserve to be. Praying often for direction and guidance, my aunt told me to try harder to mature, explaining that

God would bless me as long as I figured out His will and did it. She promised to help me understand what He expected from me.

I enrolled in college and moved in with two other Christian girls. We wall papered the ceilings of our bedrooms with outer space wall paper and exercised our independence. Although my parents were paying for school and rent, I felt very grown up. I went home every weekend for church though, where my aunt continually told me how wrong it was for a woman to go to school. She talked about the divine role of a woman to have children and be a wife. Scolding me for wasting time, she insisted that when I found a husband, my degree would be worthless. Classes seemed longer and longer. I found myself closing my eyes instead of taking notes and then, making excuses not to go to class at all. Eventually, I just pulled the shade to block out the sun and slept silently in the black bedroom beneath a ceiling full of stars.

It was under the guise of one day serving Jesus as a church-going wife and mother that I dropped out and moved home, depressed and hopeless. *If God wants me married, why isn't he sending a husband?* Then Gregg came to visit my mom. He was only five years older than me, and he was a Christian. When wind of his visit reached my aunt, she began claiming God had sent him for me. He had a beautiful Saab, a beautiful smile, and a perfect body. I was saved. God had sent me a husband. Within months of our first date, we were talking about getting married.

Leaning against the counter wearing a charcoal gray suit under a long, wool trench coat and holding two dozen red roses, he proposed to me. He seemed incredible, but I stood hollow, looking at him, thinking I couldn't feel the joy of the moment because I didn't deserve to have him. I thought he was a gift, a bridge to take me to the place God was expecting me to go. *I can finally stand beside a man and have some kids and be who God wants me to be,* I thought.

Unfortunately, the planning of the wedding lasted longer than our marriage. The long hours of my first night as a wife were spent enduring his intermittent bouts of senseless screaming. I curled up on the hotel bed in my gown wondering how I'd missed this horrible, abusive part of Gregg. His violent anger became worse from the first night on, making it impossible to hide. After only a few months, I filed for divorce. Speaking out caused a huge problem, which required me to face the jeering church members, who condemned me for leaving him. Gregg was so good at hiding his ugly side that no one believed the things I was saying about him. They told me I didn't have "grounds for a divorce." I tried to keep it together, but couldn't. I would try harder in the future.

I felt like a failure. Completely alone in the world and on the outside of every conceivable life, I was shunned for a year in my church. My time was spent in hushed servitude and penance for divorcing until I felt drawn to a man who seemed perfect. I thanked God for Tony, who had gone through his own divorce. We related to each other's past mistakes, traditional family values, and strict Christian backgrounds. When he wrapped his arms around me, I lost myself in his golden brown eyes and the soapy scent of his skin. I felt hidden and safe, rescued from humiliation. He made me believe I was beautiful, and I knew he was telling the truth when he said I could trust him. He was so amazing and strong; he took care of me, and in our limited way, we loved each other. By our first wedding anniversary we had a daughter, by our second we had a son.

I was determined to make Tony happy just like my mom did for my dad. But if I tried to make plans to go somewhere or do something, including inviting people over to our house, he invariably complained about the cost of the plans I had made. His irritation filled me with feelings of inadequacy, and I grew to dread his slightest disappointment. Keeping the few friends I had at a distance allowed me to make excuses and cancel arrangements, which helped to keep the peace. Smiling through the pressure of living up to being the partner I thought he wanted, I was thinly stretched, sometimes snapping on my children when they messed up my pretty picture of a wife.

Trying to be the perfect husband, he was conscientious in doing the yard work, taking out the trash, and running our house, all of which worked together, making it very easy for me to live in a sleepy coma. He and I went on for years, both trying to be good at the jobs of husband and wife.

The only thing that energized me at all was earning my way back into good graces at church: teaching Sunday school, writing and directing the holiday programs, working with the women's outreach, and singing in the music ministry. I had notebooks filled with my aunt's teachings about spirits of death, drunkenness, fear, heaviness, depression, anger... everything. Nora taught that the devil infiltrated people's lives through evil spirits, saying demons were responsible for the bad things people did. I thought she was gifted and insightful as she thundered on about the wrath of God and His jealousy. Strutting across the stage screaming Hebrew words and their meanings at us, she explained how, in Greek, verses meant something very different. She was powerful and intimidating, and she had a stress aggravated illness, so to upset her even slightly with questions could disrupt the work of God. I was afraid of being controlled by demons, and I was afraid of being cursed by God for breaking His rules.

At the church, the congregation was cautioned against having friends or even family closely involved in our lives, as evil spirits were believed to transfer from one person to another. The doctrine appealed to our lack of hospitality and further isolated us. When my aunt told me to stay away from Amy, I couldn't take anymore. She was my sister, my best friend; we'd been through everything together. I was willing to risk it all because if God didn't want me around my sister, then I was in Hell already.

Amy and I began studying the *Bible* without the filtered interpretation of my aunt. On our own, we also read a number of books about unhealthy churches. We found that our church had cult-like tendencies and false doctrines. Together with our mom, we mustered the strength to approach Nora with our concerns. Our questions, even coming from concerned and loving family, turned my aunt into what we feared she was, a tyrant. She refused to answer anything and claimed evil would befall us for casting doubt upon her.

Within days of Nora's evil prophesy, my brother was accidentally stabbed in the eye with a screwdriver at work. He lost his sight after several painful surgeries. Nora approached me about his misfortune. She pointed her finger in my face and told me a curse would not come without a cause. "God," she claimed, "took Rich's eye to punish someone." Narrowing her stare, she peered over her glasses at me, adding, "Someone who stuck *her* finger in

God's eye by questioning His prophet." Our entire family was told to leave and never come back. Just like that, after fourteen years, we were out of the cult-church and being shunned by the only people left in our lives.

The quiet sweeping of offenses under the rug I'd practiced all of my life dominated my response to the cult-church members. If my mom, sister or I said anything to anyone, my dad and brothers were quick to reinforce the family tradition, demanding silence regarding the whole situation. Receding away from confrontation and emotionally paralyzed, I again found staying awake to be the most difficult task of every day.

Being cut from my church, I flailed and fought, drowning in the insecurity of a world I'd hidden from for so long. Clinging to a tiny bit of Christian truth forced me to painfully acknowledge my inner Pharisee. I identified myself with the ones who had torn their clothing at the words of Christ in outrage at how He had broken their rules, rules they attributed to God. It was chilling to wonder how many people felt justified in rejecting Jesus because of what they had seen in me. I placed the blame for my misguided spiritual life squarely on the shoulders of organized religion, vowing never to go to church again. I decided there was nothing beyond the simple fact that Jesus died to pay for my sins. I had what I needed to make it into heaven, but if God wanted to "save" anybody else, He would have to do it without me.

With a defense strategy and sufficient scapegoat, I had all but closed the door on my soul. There was, however, an unexpected bonus to my disgruntled rejection of Big Christianity; I was willing to validate people's angry accusations against believers. Because I was once one of the ugly Christians myself, I could say I knew what they meant. I had been judgmental and self-righteous. I could give a perspective from the other side, which proved to be disarming. I was surprisingly at ease discussing my current faith, strong but limited, and my former hypocrisy.

This was the undeniable priming to prepare me to respond differently in confrontation and friendship than ever before. It was a time when I felt so far from God I couldn't dream of being found, as if the track ended at the cliff's edge and my life had derailed with the Jesus train into the dusty red canyon below. For too long, I'd sat among the twisted wreckage waiting for someone to rescue me, but when we moved to Westbury I started over. *If life is a journey, I can change my course,* I thought. I would get back on a track.

I had no way of knowing when I saw an enthusiastic family of six moving in across the street from me, a new Johnny was about to begin. The change would slowly open an understanding, which at times threatened to overwhelm me. It seemed to be a process of large and small "light bulb" moments I seized and allowed myself to be disrupted by.

Chapter 4

Acceptance:
Am I Being Poisoned?

Andrea

Dragging the heavy bag of potting soil toward my front porch, I noticed Kimberly on the step in front of her own house assessing her empty window boxes; we both had the same idea for how to spend the morning. The tulips were already finished blooming, and the pink flowers were giving way to green leaves on the crab apple trees in my yard. I began filling my black metal planters with begonias and coleus.

"Hey," Kimberly shouted, "I have a little questionnaire to show you."

"Bring it over," I answered with a backwards wave. "I'll put some biscuits in the oven." Deciding to make the most of the last quiet week before summer break, I ran in to make a pot of coffee, luring Kimberly to stay.

Skillfully presenting an argument for why Jesus would be a democrat if He lived in our country during our time, Kimberly had a short list of policy questions written on notebook paper. Grabbing the page from her hand, I shouted on about pro-life and personal responsibility. Kimberly charged back undeterred with social and environmental issues. The heated debate, complete with waving hand gestures and condescending tones-of-voice, kept us unaware of an interested spectator inside the house. Earlier in the morning our builder had sent over a drywall repairman for some touch ups. He had spread his tarp in the hallway above the open foyer, which led into the kitchen. He very quietly smoothed over seams and bumps, silently "fixing" the same nail-pop for almost two hours. Kimberly slapped her hand over her mouth as I giggled and pointed to the steel-toed boots I could see peeking over the landing.

He must have realized we noticed him because within minutes, he was in the kitchen with an amused look on his face. He wanted in on our discussion; we could tell by the way he surveyed the room, eyeing us up. Shoving both hands into his overall pockets, he looked past us to a point on the ceiling and began explaining how he and his wife couldn't agree on a church to attend. Shaking my head in disbelief, I glanced at Kimberly as the man asked for advice. Before leaving, he offered his opinion on Jesus' political affiliation. Laughing and quoting us, he pointed to me as the conservative one and to Kimberly as more liberal.

Kimberly

Our discussions always ended when Tony came home. I had been aware of the odd shift of disposition from the time we met, but it became apparent to me that afternoon when Tony walked in as Andrea and I sat laughing about the drywall man. At the sound of the garage door going up, she stood and hurried to the sink; I watched her morph back into a wife. When we talked, she was so alive and vibrant and knowledgeable, but I noticed how different her face looked watching her smile a hello in his direction as he came through the door. *Did the clock just strike twelve?* I picked up my mug to shield it from a spray of lemon scented cleaner, as she wiped off the counter. Asking about his day, she turned to adjust the heat under the pot on the stove. Even though the conversation was not especially captivating, I stayed despite the uncomfortable nature of observing Andrea trying to balance her desire to live her own life and her role as a wife.

Andrea

I couldn't believe Kimberly didn't excuse herself when Tony came home. It was hard concentrating on what we were saying. When my husband was home, I was a wife. I didn't talk on the phone or go anywhere. I cooked and cleaned and did wife or mom things, not friend things. A wave of relief crashed over me when Tony changed into dumpy clothes to prep the riding mower for the season. After he walked out, I leaned on the counter and realized I'd sprayed my coffee with antibacterial kitchen spray, so I poured it in the sink.

I could tell Kimberly sensed the strain, and I was worried it might make her uncomfortable. Trying to act natural, I began telling her about Noah, a baby I'd lost. The morning we were going to bury him, Tony's parents showed up at our house. It was shocking to open the door to the two of them standing on the porch; neither Tony nor I ever dreaming they would come. They were never very sentimental, not even a tiny bit. After having coffee and a doughnut, Tony's father announced, "We'd better hit the road. We're leaving for vacation a day early." They didn't come to our son's funeral; it didn't even occur to them. I wasn't mad as much as I was sorry for Tony, but I knew his parents. Arriving in Myrtle Beach on schedule was all they could think about.

I offered excuses for them without wondering why *I* acted the way *I* acted. I never asked myself why I didn't tell them to stay or encourage them to come to the funeral. They saw me smiling, waving goodbye that day, never knowing how rude and insensitive I thought they were being.

Kimberly

She felt sad for Tony? She wasn't mad at how she was treated? It was as if she had no emotion for herself, only for others. I've been told burying a child is one of the worst life experiences imaginable. How did she endure it without ever considering her own needs? Smiling and waving good-bye as they drove off had to have pierced her already broken heart. *She must be the strongest woman I have ever met or, in her mind, the smallest.* I wanted to pick her up and stand her on the tallest mountain I could find and shout at her to claim it! I wanted her to run into the game, to stop sitting on the sidelines waiting for the coach to send her in and her tell what to do. She spoke brilliant prose and deep congruent thoughts. Her food rivaled that of top restaurants. She debated with passion. *Why didn't that translate out into the rest of her world?* I thought about walking into their garage and asking Tony if he realized any of it. I wanted to do something to infuse Andrea with confidence, so I brought up the topic of having a stronger self-esteem.

Andrea

The more Kimberly talked about self-esteem the more, for the first time ever, I was willing to wonder if it were something different from the deadly self-love I had been taught to fear. I was open to hear her explain, and I read a book she recommended. With all the talk of self, the feeling of cheating on God threatened me with thoughts of Hell and blasphemy. It was a four-lettered word to me. Self had been bashed and beaten in the *Bible*; self was at odds with God. *Self is the evil flesh me that keeps pulling toward sin.* I was supposed to die to self, and esteem others above self; what on Earth would I do if I had to quit fighting self? I thought of all the teachings along the lines of how worthless I was apart from Christ. He had value, and I only had value as I lived serving Him by serving others. I could endure anything as long as I believed it was what God would want. Having never focused on what I would need or want, I had a difficult time understanding how God could fit in with that viewpoint.

There were many days I walked around dizzy wondering if Kimberly were poisoning my mind with foolish nonsense, but I had to know the truth. I could not deny if I valued myself *at all* I would say and do things very differently and would have from the very beginning. I tried to think if I had ever heard a single healthy word in church about self, and I was left with a realization. There was an apparent lack of distinction between having self-esteem and being self-centered or selfish. *Were they two separate concepts?* It was a lot to consider.

At times, I felt a calm resolution, a peace knowing even if words failed me in explaining why I believed something; I still knew I believed it. Then there were times, even when I felt I had adequately defended my reason for thinking a certain way, I later had the nagging thought, *Maybe Kimberly was right*. Many times I realized she was. That was part of the authenticity for me. I had to admit when I was being swayed while fighting the urge to agree for the sake of unity.

Kimberly

I tried to agree or at least listen to her explanations about self-esteem and God. Sometimes the distance between the two seemed so far apart that I thought, *God must want us all to be deprived and emotionally dysfunctional.* I knew having self-esteem was not a bad thing, but telling a Christian to think of herself, even sometimes, felt like a dabbling into the dark side. The dark side was not so fun. I'd been there. But I had to learn more about her world, and how she came to believe living an oppressive life was a way to exist.

I had to admit, I felt an agitation at the mention of God, as if He were atop mountain I couldn't seem to climb. Church was the broken harness failing to hoist me to an understanding of Him because holier-than-thou and rigid were not things I wanted to believe in or identify with. How could religious people act as if they actually knew something about a god no one had ever seen?

I was really good at denouncing God with all my research and love of a good debate. I understood human origin, and it had nothing to do with some story about Creation. I'd been to the museums and seen evolution.

I'd read articles and scientific journals. They were there to look at, examine, and believe. With God, I couldn't recognize Him or find any of the confirmation I needed. I couldn't come to terms with destructive behavior, abuse, or the general malice we have as people toward one another.

But as I held my children at night, I could sense the God I questioned during the day. It was inescapable; the love was too powerful to come from nothing. Holding each of them, I would cry tears of joy and stroke their beautiful faces and smell their hair knowing they were not just here by chance. I wanted to...needed to resolve this uncertainty.

If she had a huge need for self-esteem, I had a need for a God I could understand. The connection was still missing for me. I felt nothing but listened intently to the way Andrea described knowing God in her life, like she could rest in Him. I didn't tell her how I'd done a great amount of reading trying to figure it all out. I just kept asking the questions, and she continued answering, though not always as scholarly as she would have preferred.

On a warm morning at the beginning of summer, over omelets with extra tomatoes, I looked Andrea directly in the eye. I wanted to see if she would flinch. I wanted to see in her the questions I was certain were there. I asked with a slight smile, "So, tell me, do you really believe Jonah was swallowed by a whale or that a man had an ark full of animals? Doesn't that sound ridiculous?"

"Yes it does," she said, frowning. "I know it sounds ridiculous, but I believe it. I believe all of it." She was so confident and sure. I was amazed. Andrea's faith seemed so solid and without question. I wanted that faith but could never overcome the nagging questions Andrea never even seemed to ask. "The *Bible* is true, for example," she continued, "God gave Eve one of Adams ribs and that's why a man has one less rib than a woman."

Did she just say that a man has one less rib? "Andrea," I leaned in and whispered, "No they don't."

The confidence went to blank as she uttered, "A man and woman have the same number of ribs?" I nodded completely baffled she believed they did not. I stopped firing off questions realizing I'd stumbled into awkward territory. My debate was to underscore my need for answers not to corner a friend, but I had.

"Huh." She muttered, "I guess it took me 34 years to learn that one." She looked as if she'd been kicked in the stomach. Breakfast was over pretty quickly, and we arrived back home just in time to keep me from showing Andrea how close I was to tears. I knew she was embarrassed, but I also knew it had nothing to do with her. It was my disgusting cynicism driving me into an attack machine. I walked around everyday looking for the answers to Jesus. Although Andrea struggled with religion, she had a firm belief in God. I needed to experience God personally, not just hear about Him from some priest or through a verse that sounded like a foreign language. I needed answers. Shutting myself in my bedroom, I sobbed on my hands and knees, "I want the relationship she has with her God, centered on Him no matter what questions arise or the ridiculousness of the story."

Andrea

The drive home was awkward for me. Once I stopped speaking from my heart and started listing things I'd heard, I said something pretty stupid. I took anatomy in school, and I did well enough to know there are 206 bones in the human body. Telling Kimberly the book of Isaiah in the

Bible says the Earth is round should have been enough.

She thought I was confident in my "religion," but all I really had was faith in God's existence and a belief that my eternal life depended upon Jesus. I was coming up just as short as she was, just in different areas. In showing my weakness, I was being genuine, even when it embarrassed me.

Kimberly

I heard a knock at the door taking me from the isolation of my bedroom. I had forgotten my appointment with the cable company to fix our outage from the night before.

The repairman quietly busy, I kept replaying our breakfast conversation in my head; it was like watching a bad made-for-TV movie, and I was the villain. I was the Joan Collins of my own *Dynasty*. The repairman interrupted my daze probably trying to make small talk with the crazy woman who was staring at him from the kitchen table, "If you don't mind my suggestion, I have to tell you…"

He has to tell me what? I wondered in irritation, wanting to continue on in my distraction.

"Do you listen to the radio a lot when you drive?" He smiled.

"Yes," I said. *Do I look like I care?*

"Then, you gotta listen to 96.5 on the radio. It will change your life. It changed mine," he promised.

It will change my life? Who would believe this? I contemplated, walking to the driveway irritated that I was intrigued enough to go listen. As I sat in my car, I tuned the radio to 96.5. It was the Christian radio station for our area. The first song I heard was 'Open the Eyes of my Heart.' The tears fell once again, and I knew sitting in that smoldering car with the windows rolled up and the radio softly playing, that God somehow...was there.

Andrea

Kimberly told me the radio story, and I was seeing two sides of her, which took remarkable genuineness on her part. She easily could have stayed hardnosed, adamantly questioning the validity of the Christian God. At times she did, very seriously, debate the possibility that religion was a made up security blanket, a coping mechanism for people who needed it. It was a cool position, one which sounded educated and showed Kimberly capable of critical thought processes. She could have hidden behind those arguments, letting the other side of her wallow in the unacknowledged darkness, but she didn't. Instead she showed the whole, seemingly convoluted picture. She struggled out loud in front of me and listened while I struggled in the same way with both sides of myself.

Kimberly

Meeting a Christian who became my best friend seemed like an ironic gift from God. *Did He have a sense-of-humor?* Andrea applied the words of the *Bible* in common language and matter-of-fact tones. Listening to her explain her views on Jesus, she emoted a calm resolve that was contagious. I started to see through my examination the possibility that God was not just there, He wanted to be a part of my life. I opened a *Bible* for the first time since college. Almost 15 years had past. Reading from *The Message*, I took my questions to the pages.

Andrea

As we both sifted through the soil of our souls to better understand who we were, our tried-and-true rationalities were becoming even less reasonable. We were digging out, disposing of preconceived notions as we went further into our beliefs while uncovering some of the darkest moments of our lives. Over and over, we were met with the question of why; *why do I think this way? Why do I act this way? Why do I believe this way?* Each conversation was an opportunity to reinforce a growing desire to find an adequate explanation for our choices and to strengthen the bond of our friendship.

Chapter 5

Testimony: Seeing Behind the Curtain

Kimberly

Someone once asked me if I were an animal what animal I would be. I easily responded, a zebra. On its exterior there are two opposing surfaces, one white as an angel and one black as darkness.

Growing up, Sunday's were routinely spent singing hymns at the Presbyterian Church then hurrying over to my Grandparent's kitchen. For the first two years of my life, my parents lived with them; I know I was the most loved baby in the world. My Grandma was a devoutly religious woman who came over from Scotland at the age of 16 and lived in the Salvation Army barracks. When I slept over at her house, she would sing "Jesus Loves Me" and make me kneel beside the frilly rose scented bedcovering to pray.

I'd peek to see her still mumbling and worry I'd finished too soon. My grandfather, born in 1901, worked in the light bulb factory with Thomas Edison, who he called an, "old man," told stories of swimming in the Hudson River between East Orange, New Jersey, and Manhattan. He was so insightful, never saying a bad word about anyone, and telling me race, gender, wealth, none of it mattered compared to your heart.

The oldest of three, my younger sister and brother and I had a traditional Midwest family upbringing. We enjoyed all the luxuries of summer vacations, big birthday parties, Santa and the Easter bunny. My father, who had been in the military, provided the steady life of a postal worker. He was dependable, loyal, and disciplined doing things like rolling coins on the living room floor, or mapping out our next big vacation on notebook paper. If some fathers are entrepreneurs, mine was an adventurer. He wanted to drive our family of five to a different location each summer and try to hit all 48 states; we made it to 42. I remember my father, waking us all up at 4 am in the back seat of the car and yelling, "Get out...get out!" He had pulled off the barren freeway and parked in some farm field. He was gleefully running around the car; we'd made it to Kansas and wouldn't be passing through on the return home. We had to "touch ground." It was state 36.

My stay-at-home mother, who would iron clothes in front of our only television set and talk to PTA moms on the clunky pea green phone hanging on the wall, eventually rode the late 70's wave of bra burning revolutionaries. Doing the dishes shaking her hips, she would sing out while Helen Reddy's *I am Woman* played on the stereo. She'd croon, "Oh, yes I am wise, but it's wisdom born of pain...I've paid the price, but look how much I've gained."

She went to nursing school when I was 13 and became an LPN. I could sense something in her changed, but I didn't know what.

My parents had no addictions, peculiar behaviors, or horrible arguments that I witnessed. I never got spanked. We ate dinner as a family together every night, and I was taught the importance of a good education. They forced me to go to church, which I hated preferring to sleep; however, it was a small pay-off for the good food that followed at my grandparent's. I was aware many girls did not have what I had as divorces were on the rise, and the dawn of talk shows left me wondering if everyone in America had a weird uncle. I didn't.

We looked perfect and wanted to be, but we weren't. My parents loved by showing or doing but were somehow afraid of speaking of love directly. It resembled the feeling I had in junior high, when I was forced to slow dance with my older male cousin at a family wedding. We knew we could, but it felt so awkward, we'd rather not. We lived seemingly paralyzed in displaying or speaking of our emotions. I knew they loved me, but I felt this reserve, which unfortunately at times, left me questioning if something was wrong with me. My parents were the best at showing, but not so great at the telling, and sometimes, I just needed to hear the words.

The choice of parenting style my dad imposed on me, his first born, unintentionally added to my feelings. He called himself a "realist." If I ever thought I was good at something, he made sure to point out the thousands of others who were better. Although he did this out of love, it presented as a constant reminder I wasn't as good as other children who may have been trying harder or practicing more. Because we did not share emotions, I believed he valued me if I was successful, even though he never seemed to confirm any of my successes. If angered, he motivated me well by occasionally offering a shadowy prediction that I would never amount to anything in life. By telling me I was "going down the wrong road," he hoped I would get back in line and try harder. He was right, every time.

My father, the realist, never realized the down side of his philosophy. It left me never content in the moment for just who I was. I could always be better, so I struggled with felling satisfied. I was never quite good enough; therefore, *I* wasn't good enough. There was always more I could do or say or become. I could tell he felt the same way about himself, but I didn't know how to express my feelings, so I never asked why. We were fine. Sometimes the pressure felt almost too much to bear, and I would simply want to be the most loved little girl in the world again.

Dance was how I escaped. It was my religion of choice. My dance teacher, MaryAnn Demare, a former Radio City Music Hall Rockette, had opened a studio in my town when I was a young girl. She told my mom and dad I had "natural" talent and always positioned me front row center. I loved the sweating, physical exertion of rehearsals, the lights of the stage, the sounds of music filling an auditorium, and even the smelly leather dance shoes. I traveled the country a few times every year attending workshops and dance competitions, spending most afternoons at the studio helping out in other classes and taking lessons. I was being groomed to become a professional.

My grandma already thought I was. She would tell all the ladies at church I was a professional dancer and she wouldn't lie because she was at church. The church ladies would run and hug me and congratulate me on being a professional dancer. Grandma never understood the difference between dance competitions and Broadway. It was all professional to her.

I spent most of my junior high years dancing at the studio after school determined to be the best. By high school, successful in my attempts at dancing and surpassing my competition, I made good on the first born over-achiever label, but cracks were starting to show. Between lead roles in the school plays, singing in the church choir, and National Honor Society grades, I got drunk most weekends and had a lot of wild nights partying. It was my secret life, my escape.

I also learned how easy it was to receive the validation I craved from a guy. Although drawn to it, this lifestyle was not always what I was expecting. Sometimes, it was hell. He was 22. I was just 16. It doesn't take much alcohol for a young girl to find herself on a boat sailing to some cabin out in the middle of nowhere and taken to a bedroom. I never said no; I never said yes. I was just there, mostly conscious. Other than my friend who was with me, I never told anyone. That would have been shredding the façade my parents counted on. I wasn't going to be the child who unveiled the big elephant in the room.

Traveling to New York City over Valentine's weekend of my senior year with my mom, I was set to audition at a few dance schools. Adelphi University was a small liberal arts college with a fabulous dance program. Walking around the bustling campus, I was elated with what I saw. Alive with anticipation, girls in pink tights stretching against the park benches in their leg warmers let us know we were close to the auditorium. During the audition, the instructors postured around with huge wooden sticks chanting "...more...give me more..." I could thank my father for teaching me to do great things under pressure; I thrived in that environment. My heart pounded as the head master marched up and down the line one inch from every dancer's face, "...no...no...yes, you're in,...no."

He came up to me. I hoped my sweat beads wouldn't fall on his nose as we stood almost eye to eye. His breath smelled of cigarettes and coffee, "...yes, you're in..." I was accepted on the spot. When the line torture was over, I walked into the corner and dry-heaved into my dance bag. It was the purging of 12 years of training which seemed to come down to one audition. I'd made it. I was going to New York to dance.

No one would have guessed I was such a mess internally, on the brink of disaster. I was wedged between two worlds and they were about to collide. Just weeks before I was to leave to study dance in New York, I contracted mono so severely that my doctor sent me directly to the hospital. Lying emaciated in the hospital bed, I knew I was down the wrong road my father had warned about. The parties, the passing around of drinks, and the late nights out had taken their toll. The balding doctor walked into the room and without looking up from the chart, reported, "Kimberly, I don't think you are going to be able to leave for college next week." He waited through my long pause that probably told him I couldn't comprehend what he was saying. His furrowed brow sank low to his eyes, "Your pancreas is very swollen. You cannot dance for six weeks without risking a rupture. You'll have to wait until the January semester. You need to relax and get your strength back." I looked through him in utter silence, watching the scene in my mind of my dream slipping away.

Afraid to move, I closed my eyes hoping when I opened them, it would all be over. I'd worked my whole life striving for New York. My mom walked bedside, and for a moment, I felt myself reaching toward her to save me. We stayed silent, the emotions were too uncomfortable. After she left, I cried alone on the cold, steel framed bed knowing I had no one to blame but myself. The night dragged on without a visitor, a call from a friend, my father...or God.

As the first born, I felt the unspoken pressure from my parents to be successful, so in a convoluted way, they could prove to the world, *We're not that bad...look what we made.* I could see it in their eyes. They wanted me to become someone, so I never wanted to disappoint them. I felt from my earliest memory, my job, my role, was to be their validation. So as I lay crying, I sobbed, *They're holding their hopes in me, and I am not measuring up.*

Weak and tired, after being discharged from the hospital, I needed a stress relief, so I decided to make the most of a boy I'd met a few weeks prior, Brad. He was fun and warm, a person who could make me laugh for hours, and that worked like medicine for me. I was in limbo, hoping the five months until January would pass by quickly.

In December, just weeks before I was scheduled to leave, my life changed forever. I carried my little jar into the dirty community clinic on Market Street, the street where no one would know me because it was in a bad section of town. Terrified, I waited with Brad down the street at a phone booth while the sample was tested. Neither of us spoke, even when I stepped out of his beat-up, junk car with a quarter in my hand. Shivering, I dialed the number the clinic nurse had given me.

The woman who answered sounded like a preschool teacher, "Honey, its positive. You are pregnant."

I held the phone to my ear until after the click, the

silence, and then a new dial tone. Gently, I placed the receiver back onto the phone and turned to Brad, who was still in the car. I didn't have to say a word.

"It'll be ok, you'll be ok," he whispered between my sobs of regret. I kept seeing my dad's face, deacon at the church, passing around the offertory plate while everyone whispered what a shame his poor daughter had turned out to be. *This can't be happening,* I thought.

I stopped praying and quit going to church with my family. I wasn't worth the trouble. Christmas evaporated around me; I didn't pay attention to anything, not a family moment, a gift, nothing. I had plenty of practice with hiding, so no one had a clue I was struggling with a difficult decision. I told no one except Brad, I couldn't bear to say the words out loud. My drama teacher from high school and my dance teacher kept calling wondering if I was excited about New York. My aunt and uncle threw me a going away party, and friends from school mailed me letters of encouragement. Everyday, I forced myself to get out of bed and pretend to live the life I was expected to have. I became a portrait of a life; a hazy smear of frantic black decisions and illusory yellow emotions.

New York was within reach, just weeks away, yet obviously, I couldn't go pregnant. I'd heard how for some women the decision comes easily, but for me, it was torture. *How could I raise a child living in my parents' home with a younger brother and sister? How could I give up my dream, my family's investment in my dancing?* Yet, I started to have instinctual feelings about being a mother and having a life growing in my body. My mind raced over all the options until I became resolved. I would have never been able to look my dad in the eye again. My mother would have died of a broken heart. My grandparents would have been mortified. Reminding myself of what the nurse told me, *It's just a bunch a cells that will eventually become a baby if you wait too long to make a decision,* I phoned the clinic and made an appointment to end my pregnancy.

I was set up in a room in a line with other girls just like me, all hoping we were making the right decision. When the nurse came in and announced the doctor would be delayed, I tensed, thinking it was God's attempt at intervention. I heard Him; I recall wanting to pull the IV out of my arm and run the hell out of there. I wanted to tell Brad I couldn't go through with it and that we could do it together one way or another. Sitting in the plastic recliner, I battled on in my mind for many hours until the doctor returned. I was first. Shutting off my emotions was habitual. I ignored God and faded away under the humming florescent tubes.

I realized, walking in my front door late that night, I had not talked to my parents all day. Seeing both of them standing in the kitchen, it was clear they were worried having no idea where I was. I had told them I would be shopping, if only that were true.

"The mall closed hours ago," my mom said, with tears in her eyes. "We thought you were dead somewhere on the road."

My dad jumped in sternly, "I told mom we'd never see you again."

"We were shopping and lost track of time," I whispered lowering my gaze taking an ambled step to the nearest kitchen chair. My eyes averted the disgusted look from my father I tried to run from my whole life. My mom looked as breakable as the holiday wishbone. I wanted to tell them I was not just goofing off. I wanted to tell them I'd just ripped my heart out and that I believed I was evil and ugly, but I did none of that. I again went to sleep alone with the pieces of me broken on my bed. I never told a single person...ever. On Sunday, like the pretty portrait of the ballerina lacing her shoes, I left for New York.

I tried for many gut-wrenching months to energize myself in New York, but I was physically depleted from the mono and emotionally depleted from the recovery of my decision. The voice of the disapproving campus doctor, who examined me after six weeks, played over in my head, *If you keep having those done, you'll never have any children.* Then, my beloved grandfather had a heart attack and my grandmother, my biggest fan, died just two months into my arrival. My parents sent for the chaplain to tell me, and he drove me to the airport to go home for the funeral. I spent the next two days alternating between sitting next to my stoic grandfather and projectile vomiting in the bathroom.

I don't even remember the flight back to New York. I slipped into loneliness. Not a need for company loneliness, but a dark, empty, lost feeling of despair; a deeper need to have back what was forever lost loneliness. Thoughts of my grandfather, now alone in his house without me there to comfort him, kept me tossing and turning. Nightmares of crying babies tormented my sleep, and many nights I needed to call Brad from the black pay phone in the dorm hallway at 3am. The depression was a hurdle I could not overcome, even though I auditioned for a show and was chosen. The line of girls auditioning stretched out the door and they chose me, but it wasn't enough to draw me out. Dancing seemed ridiculous. I wanted to go home. I didn't even recognize what road I was on anymore.

New York vanished. No one talked about it or asked why I gave it up. Everyone must have been embarrassed, or afraid of embarrassing me. Living at home, I decided to attend a local college and work toward a psychology degree. After receiving my BA, I'd go back to New York able to support myself. I had a plan.

For nearly three years, I focused entirely on my education and lived a quiet life dating Brad. I was finding strength in what I was learning at school and wanted to be happy. In time, my relationship with him began to unravel as he seemed content about his future, and I was more driven. We ended on good terms, and with that, I sensed the chapter closed on one of the darkest times of my life.

I re-entered the world of the single people. It had been a few years, but I was ready for new experiences. I made the college football dance team, found some great friends, and joined into the campus life. I was familiar with the lifestyle, excelling in activities and academics, while attending all night parties and dating. This time around, a bit smarter, I started to recognize the pattern.

From across a smoky college bar, I noticed Eddie. My friends shouted over the driving beat of the dance music blaring through the speakers, asking me if I was interested in the guy smiling in my direction. He was 6' tall and built strong like a man who ate meat and did lumberjack stuff. His hair and eyes were dark, and he had naturally tan skin from his Italian heritage. Once I walked up to the bar, there was magnetism between us, though I pretended not to notice him. Ordering drinks for my friends, I was aware of his presence drawing next to me moving into my space. As I drank in the sight of him, the noise and people seemed to vanish, and I felt myself connecting with the swaggering frat boy with amazing good looks. I knew immediately, he was the one. He knew it too.

We took classes at similar times and met for beer and

wings on campus during breaks in between. With Ed, I could be myself completely, only doing my hair and make-up if I wanted, living in his sweat pants and big T-shirts. I said what my opinions were and told him my dreams. He did the same. He would put on smooth jazz music, lighting candles, and telling me I was the most beautiful woman he had ever met. Long talks lingered on through the nights as we told each other every detail of our lives. Leaving nothing out, it was the first time I could bare my past hurts, my weaknesses, and Ed listened then shared his own. Our relationship was intoxicating.

The multi-faceted, marquise cut diamond ring Ed placed in his top dresser drawer made it one day hidden under his black jersey briefs. Intended to be saved until Valentine's Day, Ed decided January 18th was close enough and got down on one knee and proposed. I acted surprised. We'd known each other four months.

My parents were happy for us, though they were upset by my decision to switch to Catholicism and marry in the Catholic Church. Ed thought it would be best if our kids were raised in his denomination. Even though he never attended church and my family did, it felt like we'd chosen our first thing together. Having walked away from God, church was immaterial, so I didn't care. I loved the way my diamond glittered under the stained glass windows in the sanctuary.

My plan to return to New York to dance after earning my BA was foiled because Ed had longer to finish than I did in college. We wouldn't be together if I left, and he said he could never live there anyway. Dance was part of me, but inside, the past was quietly haunting, making me feel undeserving of my dream. Punishing myself, I gave it away. I loved Ed, but I *needed* his love more. Eighteen months later, I spent the entire night dancing at our wedding.

However, like everything else in my life, with all the good, there was a dark side. Ed and I had secrets, too, and I knew how to keep them. Two broken people came to be married having no idea how to change their destructive patterns or love the other. Shrewd in our ability to brag enough to confuse people, friends even asked us "how we did it" and sought our advice. It was dishonest in a political way. We smiled and told 'em what they wanted to hear.

Having lost his father suddenly at the boyhood age of six, then living his teen years under the intimidation of an alcoholic step father with a rage problem, Ed did not have the mentor every young man needs. It was an emotional cocktail that altered his awareness of what to expect in love and *in* love.

In our marriage, he became unreasonably difficult to please as he found fault in everything I did. Nothing was up to his standards and he pointed it all out as if it were my fault he wasn't happy. If I could just be a better wife, mother, housekeeper, money saver, wage earner, then *he* wouldn't have to be so hard on me. I understood the man behind the words and chose to stick it out. He wanted the picture perfect image he'd been denied as a child. I needed the prince charming to make me feel special. We were both caught up in a cycle, trying to heal the past.

Episodes of intense arguments continued off and on for years, like bad re-runs of old shows where the jokes aren't funny anymore, and the people just look silly. However, Ed and I wanted the marriage to work, so we worked hard at keeping it together. We attended couples counseling three different times and attended a marriage retreat weekend as we fought to gain control of our past tendencies. Each year, as the brutality of our arguments lessened, we were then left with the remnants of the wars. We had a lot of anger and bitterness, mixed in with the passionate love and commitment we had always possessed.

Years of marriage and four children later, we had carved out a decent life. I had left dancing all together and settled into my role as a working mother. Ed and I were successful enough to afford some luxuries and take summer vacations. Our children were good students and over involved in fun activities. The grandparents spoiled all four of them on a regular basis, and my sister and brother lived nearby offering plenty of cousins for them play with. So, when I began to feel the twinges of discontent, I was unprepared for how low I would sink.

Psychology did have its limits, and distanced from God for years, I began questioning the reason for my existence. *Was I just a bunch of cells that grew from an embryo to become a baby and eventually an adult? Why can't one drop of rain fall on Africa? Why do children suffer abuse? Why can't we just be happy?*

Ed and I had attended church only a handful of times in 11 years of marriage, four of them to baptize our children. I had the foundations of religion, but I did not have faith. I could recite some verses or prayers I memorized from childhood, but there was no meaning behind the words. It eventually caused me to be angry at even the notion of God. *Where was He...was he even there?*

I started to have anxiety. I couldn't sleep or drive alone. I hated bridges and elevators, feeling trapped and helpless to save myself if something happened. My head was in a fog all day, every day. Privately, I wondered if I were having a nervous breakdown. Doctors tried to help, but said I was "fine," and fearing horrible side effects, I wouldn't take any medication. Ed supposed it was the hormones from four past pregnancies, but I knew better. This was deeper, a stirring of my soul.

The uncertainty I felt funneled into one rainy Halloween night. I lost it after 34 years of holding it in and ran into the darkness. I cried. I fought. I screamed out all of the things I ever wanted to say but never did. The rain splashing on my face, I ran from my meaningless life hoping to find a reprieve. The gift of my four children, and the thoughts of each of them, was the only thing that kept me strong enough to eventually stop running and fall to the ground. In the thunderous pounding of heartbeats and storm, somewhere out in the middle of nowhere, I found a flicker of God. I found the courage to pray.

Praying a real prayer for the first time in years and giving my life back over to a God I wasn't sure existed, left me feeling compelled. As if the love poured on me when I was the most loved baby in the world reminded me, I deserved His attention and love. I spoke to God all the emotions and thoughts and regrets of my life as if I were plainly talking to my father. I prayed for forgiveness and guidance in turning my broken, lost soul back to Him, and for help in drudging through the questions my mind would not let rest. I begged God to have patience with me and told Him that if He was willing, I would receive and learn about Him.

Ed and I decided to build a house in Westbury just weeks later. As the builders dumped concrete for a foundation and erected planks for walls, I poured myself into books about foggy brains, anxiety, and God. I read literature on the big bang theory and evolution. I read three books written by a formerly agnostic author who made it his life's mission to answer the questions about a divine creator and ultimately Jesus Christ through painstaking investigative journalism and a trek across three continents. I relentlessly read about the tough questions I could never resolve regarding Christianity. Seeking answers, I was trying to keep the inequity at bay.

Near the end of the five month building process, we pulled up to our new life shining in the sun. Feeling the warmth emanate off the bricks, I had no idea what was about to happen as we prepared to move into our new home. I waved to the smiling woman across the street who was sitting on a makeshift ramp leading up to her front door.

Chapter 6

Church:
Getting Sucked Back In

Andrea

I thought I was happy being an ex-church goer. I enjoyed the freedom of talking about spiritual things without feeling I was enlisting people. It's always in the back of people's minds that they're being won over to something when someone mentions church. The world spun in the wrong direction as I listened to my neighbor, Gabby, pitch the idea of my family joining her family on a visit to the big, popular Baptist church in town. It felt weird to be invited, very weird. I had said I wanted to visit Old North church, but it was the kind of comment I make when I say something like, "I want to get lippo suction." Knowing I never will, I'm acknowledging a need. My first move was to beg Kimberly to come with us, which was evidence of how church brings out the recruiter in people. Nothing could have prepared me for the experience.

On July 3rd at the "traditional service," listening to the prehistoric music, Tony and I looked at each other yawning. I wanted to hate it, so I was glad the music was a little boring. Almost no one was raising their hands; it wasn't really a hand raising atmosphere. As the singing portion of the service ended, we sat down for the sermon. Looking in the bulletin, I was thinking, *Oh super, the real pastor isn't even speaking today.* The associate pastor hopped onto the stage and started with a joke. Relaxed and confident, his manner upstaged the music the way a red convertible outdraws a blue Baptist church bus. He artfully fired away about my favorite topic, The United Stated of America. Sitting on the edge of the pew drinking in every word, I closed my eyes, and at one point, it felt like a serenade. He was saying the most beautiful things about God and the history of our Country; I almost forgot to be afraid. *Don't get sucked in. They'll use you and throw you away,* I pleaded. It was too late. I was falling in love with Old North.

During the closing song, there was a guy a few rows ahead, I called him Mr. Clean because he had the cool slick bald look; he was lifting his hands. I couldn't stop looking at him, and later I asked Kimberly if she noticed. She and Ed weren't too comfortable with the hand raising. I wanted to *feel* God in my life the way Mr. Clean was feeling Him. I loved the abandon he showed sticking out in the cautious crowd. I knew God was more than an emotional experience, but I had not been in a church for six years. I suddenly realized how much I missed worshiping with a congregation. I promised myself I wouldn't do anything other than attending Sunday morning, and I was going to do whatever it took to go to the "contemporary service."

Kimberly

There was no way I was going to church. I knew I needed God, but I did not need organized religion. That came with too much baggage, and I certainly did not need any more of that. I expected to hate it or disagree with the sermon and never go back. If it weren't for Andrea, I wouldn't have gone at all. What happened was the complete opposite of my initial predictions. A sense of calm came over me as soon as my feet hit the carpet in the Worship Center. It drew me into an awareness of something beyond myself.

The pastor spoke of America and how it related to Jesus. He was funny and down-to-earth. He told jokes and wore regular clothes. The music was more upbeat than I'd ever heard in a church, with drums and saxophones and back up singers. I counted three people with their hands up praising, and it freaked me out to see such public displays of worship. I cried the entire service; everything moved me. Walking out I was counting the minutes until we could go back. It was the best day of church in my entire life.

At first, the emotions left me uneasy. It was uncomfortable to fathom the love of God on me. *Who was I?* The responsibility of knowing God felt heavy at first. I wasn't sure I could do it or even wanted to. Without God, I could be angry and blame and hide. Those were familiar things in my life. Without them, I would be exposed. It was much deeper than how Psychology understands the mind; this dealt with the soul, a soul that would live in eternity. It was the big leagues of understanding, enlightenment at the price of comfort. I would have to learn to give of myself in ways that were terrifying. I would have to rely on accountability, forgiveness, and trust, even with the questions my mind could not understand.

Ed and I went with Gabby and her husband, Phil, to a welcome dinner hosted by Old North. Going to the welcome dinner re-introduced me into the world of the church people; the ones who smile a lot, carry a *Bible*, and say *God Bless you* even when no one sneezed. We attended partly to convince ourselves we had the right church and partly to convince ourselves we didn't. We met a few of the pastors who didn't throw any of that "you need saved stuff" at us or tell us we were terrible sinners on our way to Hell if we didn't repent. They spoke of a relationship with Jesus, a *personal* relationship that could not be defined or translated through anyone else. I respected that. I certainly did not want to fit into some church mold, and I appreciated the idea of a relationship developing.

Preparing to leave, we noticed a couple and their grown son walking toward us. I recognized them as a family from my daughter's softball team. Smiling broadly, the mother greeted us saying she was glad to see us visiting. Then, out of the blue she asked, "What church did you belong to before?"

Sensing the change in demeanor I joked, "Oh, we're Catholic. Look four kids; I was a good Catholic." No laughter followed, so I broke the awkward moment, "You have how many kids?"

Lifting her head and eyebrows, she answered through a satisfied grin, "Five, we have five children."

Her need to win the contest of "most kids" caught me off guard, but I acknowledged the notion offering simple praise, "Wow, you beat us. We've definitely stopped at four."

She nodded approvingly adding that she was older than me, and some of her children were younger than my youngest. With an exaggerated wink, she made an odd comment, "Hey, think of Sarah she had a child at age 90; she did it."

I wondered who Sarah was, thinking I must have missed some People magazine article about a 90-year-old woman who had a kid. I decided to ask, "Who's Sarah?"

With her forehead wrinkled, she threw her hands up, "Sarah! You know, from the *Bible*. Abraham's wife?" She leaned into me puzzled.

"Oh, I'm sorry; I didn't know who you meant," I admitted.

She had a look of happy bewilderment asking, "You don't *know* who Sarah was? What church did you grow up in?" She forged on still leaning in, head tilted. Her piercing eyes glazed over like a tiger studying its prey. I stood there frozen, Gabby looking at me with torturous pity, wondering why this woman was so interested in what I knew.

I started sweating trying to respond despite the clear heart pounding noise in my ears, "Well," I began, "I was raised Presbyterian but switched to Catholicism when I got married."

Her grown son chuckled, smirking, "Well, you must have missed the day they talked about Sarah." He was clearly appalled at my lack of *Bible* knowledge.

Apparently feeding off the discomfort she was causing me, she asked the final gavel dropping question, "Do you know the books of the *Bible*?" I knew right then our interaction was not going to end well.

Smiling widely, I responded in the most syrupy tone I could muster, "Well, yes I do. In fact, if you have a test up your skirt I'd be happy to take it for you." Before she could reply, Ed grabbed my arm. I could feel him pulling me to leave. We waved bye-bye to the nice church lady.

Andrea

I thought it was funny when Kimberly went to the welcome dinner. I wanted to tell her to just hang in the back and enjoy the PowerPoint presentations during the next regular service. The post-dinner tree lawn discussion, back at home, with Gabby was highly entertaining. Re-enacting Kimberly flipping her wrist in the air, Gabby told me how Kimberly said the lady could whip a quiz out of her dress if she had one. Phil was laughing his infectious man-giggle.

The last service Phil and Gabby attended, just a few short weeks later, the lesson was on how we should live the L. I. F. E. of Christ: Love, Instruction, Fellowship, and Evangelism. It was catchy, and it had us joking because fellowship was all we did. None of us felt comfortable with the "E," evangelizing people for God's kingdom. We didn't want to go around *saving* people. I was sensing evangelism wasn't sitting well with Gabby, especially. So in an attempt to bring the idea back to Earth, I mentioned how E-ing was just people being themselves. "We 'E' at my house when we visit and talk," I explained. They didn't come back to church after that, and Gabby quit stopping by to join us for an occasional coffee. She must have thought I was a stealth evangelist or something. Kimberly and I started calling our morning coffee "breaking biscuits."

Thinking back to the beginning of our relationship, we speculated about how strong the fear of being associated with certain people could be. Wondering if pegging people and running from them was an instinct or a decision, we considered how she and I had almost run from each other. It was as if people reacted automatically and then resented the results of those reactions. Sitting for hours over the course of days, we discussed how people seem to be hurt and cause hurt in others, especially those they love. Kimberly talked about psychological needs and I guessed about what part of it was sinful. I couldn't deny that I had gossiped and rejected people based on first impressions and funneled myself into a *type* of person.

Every time I heard of a situation, I could see myself and other people reacting in routine ways without thinking beyond what was happening right that minute. I thought, *It's like a rat trap; touch it, and it snaps.* Noticing my brother, I saw if he became irritated, nervous, hungry... even sad over a death, he blew up in anger. If my sister felt worried, glad or even excited, she focused on possible negative outcomes, as if it were her job to predict pitfalls and keep all the hopes from getting too high.

I realized I already knew how everyone was going to behave before they did anything. It was no longer cute when I could finish someone's sentence. We were almost programmed to react without questioning what was causing the behavior or if the way we were about to respond had been a successful response in the past. We were such drones in matters of relating. Not that people were dull, but whatever our typical actions and reactions were, they never varied. We were completely predictable. In effect, I saw the evidence of people failing to truly explore the possibility of different reactions having different outcomes and different outcomes having a number of possible reactions.

It was hard to admit when I couldn't seem to change a behavior I knew wasn't good for me. I had benefited from the science of psychology and the explanations behind human behavior, but even with training and education, I had no ability to guarantee a different outcome in myself or others. Happiness or fulfillment seemed to be something to strive for, though they could never be completely attained. Statistics of therapy for marriage, anger, abuse, or drug treatment curing people were low; it wasn't working. I needed to know, *Why can't we change?*

Andrea

Although completely devoted in my faith, I couldn't deny the main problem I was having, which was reconciling the number of people I knew who were still broken and dysfunctional after being Christians for years, people I had seen and heard begging God to change them, who were not being changed. *Where is the victory? Why is my whole life about Jesus and being a Christian, and yet everything feels exactly wrong?* I had written those words in my journal yet never sought answers. I'd simply posed the questions, *Why are prayers not being answered? Why are relationships deteriorating instead of improving? What is Jesus waiting for?*

Kimberly

We noticed more and more the tendency of Christians, who were caught in the world of programmed responses, to respond with an automatic reaction of their own. They were waiting for the Jesus genie to show up, and grant them three wishes. When He didn't, they became angry and frustrated. A Christian businessman broke down in anger one evening during a group discussion we were having with some other families from our church. He was waiting and waiting for his "ship to come in," growing more aggravated and furious, while sinking further and further into debt. With outstretched arms he implored, "I've prayed so hard; what else does God want from me?" I just kept thinking, *Is Jesus a genie? Do we get three wishes?*

Andrea

At first, I was laughing about the Jesus genie, but then so many of the people I knew were hung up on "unanswered" prayers. Listening to a man talk about prayer as if it were an endless rubbing of the lamp made me sad because he was so agitated and he wanted answers.

My mom was feeling rejected and unanswered too; I wanted an explanation for her. I could see she not only had the pain of the situation she was facing but the hurt and confusion from begging God for help that wasn't coming. My dad had open heart surgery and it saved his life, but the side effects of being on the pump left him diminished mentally. We still had his funny stories and love of family, but he lost his big business savvy, which was difficult to face knowing it was such a huge part of him. It wasn't until he failed at a real estate endeavor, losing his house and savings in the process that we woke up. Filing bankruptcy was so hard on my mom, who spent months offering expectant prayers to God before we packed up her house and moved her to a rental property. Cleaning the fireplace I found spirals from a stack of notebooks. She had burned her written prayers as a symbol of offering them up to God, but nobody came to save her from losing the house. She had to go to work for the first time in thirty-seven years.

Listening to others' testimonies, I was bothered by all

the talk that implied God was simply having conversations with people. It sounded as if He were taking their orders and serving up steaming dishes of just what they thought they needed. I couldn't believe it when I heard a lady say God answered her prayer to rush her through customs quickly. When she approached the counter, "Praise God," they were short staffed and waved her on through. When was God coming to my table to take my order? *Garcon, we've been waiting for quite awhile.*

Kimberly

It became clear; the point of spiritual indictors was to encourage me to press into *truth*. I continued reading the *Bible* and discussing with Andrea our human tendency to want to formulate God or demand from Him answers. Some of us even wanted to tell God what he *should* be doing with our lives or with the lives of others, as if we could somehow manage God. Looking back over the summer, we concluded none of the things we would call signs from God were rushing us through customs, or telling us where to live, or explaining to us why things happen the way the do. They were moments our focus shifted from what we sought, to Whom we should have been seeking, to Whom we should have been trusting. Faith involved taking a leap into the unknown and giving up the control of our own lives to something greater, even without all the answers, maybe without even expecting them. Instead of demanding, and hoping, we started aiming to understand the God who was everlasting. Every time we sensed Him, it was like a breeze, air we knew was there, but could suddenly feel.

I was caught off-guard by the reality of the new perspectives because I assumed once I found God to find peace. Andrea expected in finding a greater self awareness, she would gain the confidence to live. We were both mistaken. It was disappointing to face the shortfall of our new beginnings, but we were moving closer to those ideals. Something was still hanging in the air, like a thick velvety cloud amidst a clear blue sky; the shadows of which prevented the fullness of the all-encompassing light. We had more to learn.

Andrea

Without realizing it we were cresting a hill, and the speed with which we would descend into a new understanding of truth was something neither of us could have predicted. So, as our beliefs intersected more and more, we were energized, ready to peel back the layers until we were confident we had a genuine understanding of faith in God. I was examining concepts I'd long deemed off limits to question: prayer, sin, human nature. I felt the apprehension of exploring my doubts rise with the temperature of late August. Gathering my nerve, I opened the vault where I kept my well-protected beliefs hidden, it felt as if I were exposing my most precious and fragile possession to the unforgiving elements, where it could be scorched and burned by the heat of the sun.

Section 2

Getting to the Core

Chapter 7

Gauging:
A Misguided Prescription

Kimberly

"Movie night!" Ed screamed like a big kid running through the house as our four children went thundering into the basement. Movie night at our house was one of my family's favorite things to do, so we fit it in as often as we could on the weekends. Huddling together under blankets and quilts, we waited while Ed fumbled incessantly with the gigantic remote control for his big-screen TV. He put in surround sound, and I hung long navy blue drapes over the windows. It was very cave-like, perfect for watching movies and filling up on lots of candy and popcorn. We joked about the parents who didn't feed their kids sugar, wondering if they knew the post sugar-high lull was an effective sleep inducer.

After the movie, Ed carried our youngest up to bed, as I roused the other three to sleepwalk to their rooms. While tucking the blanket under a droopy little arm, I whispered, "I'll make us some fresh popcorn." We often sneaked in our own movie after the kids went to bed.

Ed rented a movie about the seven deadly sins making me certain God had a sense of humor. The story line followed a murderer who had each of seven people commit one of the seven sins to their own death. Over crunches of steaming, hot buttered sin, it occurred to me I was overeating. Overeating was gluttony. It occurred to me I was sinning. Without going to hear it from a priest or reading it from the *Bible*, I could see my daily life as sinful when others may not have noticed. It was as if sin could be obscured by a well-dressed suburban housewife and career woman, yet occurs nevertheless.

I thought about each of them separately. *Gluttony*: I not only eat too much, I eat too fast. I want things without waiting, and I want things I don't need. *Slothfulness*: I would rather take a nap than exercise, taking the easy road whenever possible, and trying to escape maximizing any effort. *Greed*: I have more than I need, I give to myself and my family first most of the time ignoring the world around me, and I purchase things just to feel good. *Pride*: I try to impress people; I like being the know-it-all, and I want the last word in arguments. *Lust*: I used my body to catch attention. I used men to fulfill my needs, and allowed myself to be lusted upon. *Anger*: I get angry at little things that should not bother me. I've stayed angry for years at certain people, and I've screamed at my family when they didn't deserve it. I don't have envy, though, never have. I take life in whatever form God intended, and if I want something someone else has, I obtain it. I guess that goes back to greed, though.

Most of the time, those things seemed to go unnoticed in my life as sin. They were not necessarily overt and certainly were not thought of in the same way as stealing, lying, and adultery. *Could they be as wrong?* Overeating late at night was a way to de-stress, so sin had not been part of my vernacular.

Dawn came too quickly, and I was having trouble forcing myself out of bed. It hardly seemed possible we were nearly a month in to the new school year; I had still not adapted to the routine we needed to keep things running smoothly. The kids missed the bus, which meant I missed my first cup of sanity and my phone call to Andrea. I groaned at the thought of facing the cool, wet weather; it was not an enjoyable start to the day. It was the time of year when the Midwest skies still warmed up, but the wind blew cold. "Missing the bus is a sin," I yelled from behind the steering wheel. "Never do that!" My kids already thought I was crazy, and my demeanor proved them correct.

My cell phone rang, and I thought it was probably Andrea wondering why I hadn't called yet. "Kimberly," the voice from my past spoke, "it's Pam."

I smiled instantly at the sound of her voice, wondering how long it had been since we'd last spoken. "How are you? What are you up to? How's life? How's married life," I asked, excited to talk to her.

Pam and her then boyfriend, Dave, were best friends with Ed and me throughout college. We were in each others weddings and they were the Godparents of my first born daughter. The past few years, our contact was limited to holidays and the occasional evening out. Pam was a devout Catholic, always bubbly and full of life. Dave was

Mr. Personality making every night out a party, even if it were just the four of us at dinner somewhere. Together they were a mixed pair as she was so sweet and he was, well, a bit of a devil.

"I have some bad news," she said through what I knew to be tears, "we're getting divorced." I stayed quiet as she went on to tell me they both loved and cared for each other deeply but had gone off in two different directions. "He's still partying Kimberly, and I want the white picket fence. Sometimes, he doesn't even come home." My heart sank for her. She was such a good person; what would allow him to throw it all away? Pam opened the flood gates, "Last weekend, he was on a business trip and when he got back I found a pair of women's underwear in his suitcase. He can't admit it, but it's clear. He won't even look me in the eye anymore. It's all part of who Dave has always been. I'm tired of believing it's going to be 'different this time'."

We talked for awhile longer and made plans to meet for lunch the next day. I couldn't help but recount some of the sin discussions Andrea and I had been having. What would drive a man to choose drinking and partying and possibly another woman over his wife who loved him? It seemed desperate.

Andrea

After talking to Pam, Kimberly walked over with a sense of purpose. A definite shift began as she had a new alert determination to fully comprehend her faith. She grabbed her own mug from my cupboard saying, "It isn't enough for us to know we sin, we have to know *why* we are driven to do these things."

I realized we were talking again about automatic reactions and destructive life choices. At first, I shrugged off the thought and offered the standard answer of a sin nature, which I'd heard about my whole life. I caught myself though, because we were too awake to accept the buzz words and talking points that enveloped questions and sent them into space dismissed, yet unanswered.

Kimberly

"What does that even mean? Sin nature…" I wanted to know, as I wrestled with the annoyance I was feeling. "A married man tempted to engage in an affair would say he loves his wife and kids. However, he feels powerless to stop himself; but why? People are ravaged by destructive choices and when they ask, 'why can't I change?' they are told it's because of their sin nature?" I questioned mockingly. We agreed how frustrating and even absurd it was to have to accept such a dismissive explanation of a human epidemic. If we wanted practical solutions we could apply, we had to find them.

Andrea

While Kimberly questioned on in her usual way, I realized how many of the ideas I'd learned were simply eloquent ways of not really answering questions. All my life, I'd been handed the idea of sin coming from birth, without adequate explanation of how to be free. I remembered the times I'd gone to my aunt for prayer when I was desperate to be free or the counsel of my parents when I needed answers I was never really given. It was like a treasure chest full of money had been handed to me to as an explanation, but inside, the money was counterfeit. I couldn't use it to buy anything. It no longer made sense. Sin nature became a hollow concept left after I dumped the once treasured illusion into the abyss. Decisions felt beyond our control, and if people couldn't change; what good was trying?

Kimberly

I saw the bad stuff as destructive behavior and poor choices. Sinning to me was disobeying the Ten Commandments, and I didn't think people thought much about those during their daily lives. I felt people were out to seek pleasure and avoid pain, plain and simple. Sometimes, the seeking of pleasure led to destructive behaviors and poor choices. Of course, God would not approve if we were to really think about our actions, but who does? Trying to avoid the pain, wandering around looking for the pleasure, takes up all our time. The excesses of drinking, shopping, gambling, adultery, and overeating were all there for us to escape into, yet they were a temporary fix. We would have to go back for more.

Andrea

I knew we were talking about something more than the specific people involved. This was life, and somehow, we were messing it up with a frenzied, got-to-have-it-now attitude, which seemed to have the urgency of life and death. We spent the day talking about marriage and how many people experience broken relationships. Even after Kimberly went home, I couldn't stop trying to figure it out. We all seemed to be pursuing whatever we currently wanted with desperation, as if the programmed responses we were familiar with were driven by a need.

A few hours after I finished making dinner, the phone rang, "Can you come over? Now." Kimberly sounded upset.

"Are you alright?" I asked, cradling the phone with my shoulder, hopping as I forced on my shoe. "I'm walking out the door."

Kimberly didn't wait for a response. She hung up, and I sloshed through the wet sleet, hurrying across the street to her house. When I walked in, there was blood all over the counter. I turned, looking toward the powder room, where Kimberly was standing with her hand wrapped in paper towels.

Cradling her injured hand she shrugged, "I just cut my finger really bad." Gesturing to the knife on the wooden cutting board in the kitchen, she grumbled, "I sliced right through my finger."

I balled up the bloody paper towels from the floor and on the counter. There were kitchen rags and a bath towel all thrown down to wipe up the mess. "Do you need to go to the emergency room?" I asked. "There's so much blood."

"That's why I called you," she answered, lifting the towel back so I could check the finger.

"Oooh," I groaned, knowing she would never go to the hospital, "you need a stitch or two."

"Thank God there was a roll of paper towels there. I was in a panic," Kimberly said, opening a first aid kit, which clearly told me she'd decided to fix it up herself. Taking it from her, I reached in and found what I thought she needed. Dabbing some cream onto a piece of gauze to help numb the finger, I offered to wrap it.

As I wound the tape around her bandaged finger, Kimberly sighed, "I just kept squeezing my hand in the paper towels until they were drenched and then grabbing more, a new handful."

By the time Ed came in, we'd cleaned up the mess. I was sure she was going to be fine, so I walked home. Kimberly's words stayed with me all evening, *I was in a panic...just grabbing more...* Thinking about reacting to a wound, I held my hand to my chest and pressed, as if futilely applying pressure to a larger, life-threatening injury. I imagined trying to stop the bleeding with anything that looked capable of making it better, gauzing up the blood. *If we were bleeding out from within, would we be willing to grab whatever we could find to pack the wound, fighting for life?*

Poor choices to drink too much or to date while married were like tiny squares of gauze, too small to have any real impact on the *wound*, but reached for anyway. Once it became clear our *gauze* wasn't helping, it would be discarded as a saturated rag, just thrown to the ground. I wondered if people and things were being pursued in the hopes that by applying them with enough pressure, the wound would begin to heal. Every one of us was frantically trying whatever was available, believing we could find something with the power to stop the wound from killing us.

Kimberly stopped by the next day after having lunch with Pam. Her mind was completely wrapped up in what was happening to her friends, surprisingly mine was too. Pouring a cup at the counter, I tried to explain the gauze illustration to ease her stress. I said, "Think of Dave in terms of packing a wound with gauze. Maybe that's what he was doing. He felt overwhelmed with work and under appreciated at home so he went out after a long day to have some drinks." Pressing on my chest, I went on about how he gauzed up the exhaustion and stress by sitting in a bar indulging in what he thought he needed. He held the drinks, the other women, the dark bar atmosphere to the wound trying to numb away the thoughts of work and Pam's disappointment in him. Once the gauze of alcohol was soaked, he threw it down, guilted by its insufficiency.

The wound still bleeding, he'd be forced to try something else, so he picked up the gauze of "family man." He turned into super spouse pressing on the inadequacies he felt as a husband. Trying to extract forgiveness and ultimately admiration from her, he believed it would make being home worth-while, make him worth-while. All while telling himself, "If she could love me enough and appreciate me enough, I could be a better husband." But that gauze wouldn't have sustained the inadequacy bleed either, so he'd begin to feel his sacrifices were going unnoticed. He'd focus on work piling up or his tired wife and think he just wanted some fun. He would think he deserved it. With the gauze of family saturated, he'd be dying, urgent for something to pack into the wound. Feeling overwhelmed at work and underappreciated at home, he again would turn to the gauze of alcohol; the cycle continues.

Kimberly

I thought of my psychology courses and how this cycle was classic and easily identifiable, but as Andrea talked; I could feel the desperation of not just Pam, but also of Dave. He seemed empty inside with no idea where to turn. I was taught there were emotional reasons behind self-addictive behaviors, and I could recognize that; however, the frenzied notion of the behaviors intrigued me. I understood for the first time how overeating or over-shopping or living a party lifestyle were somehow frantic attempts at self preservation. The desperation, the perpetual bleeding out, could be momentarily slowed with a well made pair of shoes, a pint of ice cream, or in Dave's case, another woman. Gauzing was any distracting, indulgent behavior we'd engaged in to escape the empty reality of our lives. Inevitably, the gauze would become saturated forcing us back into the addictive patterns of needing more, bigger pieces, to keep from bleeding to death.

After talking about gauzing a wound, I started to notice how this grasping seemed to dictate many of *my* decisions. I would gauze to feel better or find relief from the prevailing need always lurking in the back of my mind. My behaviors were so patterned, so predicable; there was no thought behind them. *How could eating an entire bag of chips or buying something I really didn't need be gauzing up a wound I was unaware of having?* However, the picture of bleeding out kept surfacing in my mind as I watched myself attempt to feel better with food or shopping.

I thought of the gauze scenario as a template, a predetermined outline I could use to fill in a name, need, and subsequent behavior to fill the need. It was a predictable, misguided prescription we were all writing ourselves.

State your name: Kimberly
Unfulfilled need: unconditional love
Diagnosis: unworthiness
Gauze of choice: overeating

State your name: Dave
Unfulfilled need: self-worth
Diagnosis: insecurity and fear
Gauze of choice: alcohol and attention

This prescription flooded my mind every time I saw one of the patterned behaviors materialize in my life. I was gauzing constantly, a sort of self medicating through things, while walking around with that sucking chest wound. It was shocking and embarrassing. *Why was I so needy? Why were any of us?*

Andrea

Spending many nights awake in bed picturing the misguided prescription of my own life, I'd caught myself repeatedly reaching for things and relying on people to make me feel better. I also thought about my family and friends whose behaviors could easily fit into the template. It could be excessive spending, overeating, binge drinking, or any behavior that left us numbing out and escaping into a momentary happiness or even just a distraction. The world started to look like a triage, and I found myself noticing the walking wounded around me: my husband, children, siblings…

Growing up in church, I'd learned how sinning was giving into temptation. It was presented as a clear choice to obey God or become the god of your own life, but with gauzing in mind, I saw how powerless human beings were against their desires. The things I'd been tempted to do when I was younger were no longer alluring to me, such as having sex with someone other than my husband or drinking myself into a stupor. I felt pleased with my morality and considered myself progressing toward holiness, yet as the delivery men carried the separate pieces of my new dining room set into my house, it was clear I had replaced those temptations with others less obvious.

Chapter 8

The Saddler:
I Don't Drink and Run
Around Like That

Andrea

After a long cold night, I was awakened by the crispness of the fall air squeezing through the window edges. Tony had a rule about waiting until November to turn on the heat. Although we were a few days away, I decided to touch the forbidden thermostat and adjust the controls. Kimberly arrived a bit late for coffee, and I was hoping the house would heat up given the extra time.

Opening the door, I asked, "You're wearing mittens?"

"I had to dig them out of the closet," she joked. "No offense, but I got frostbite sitting in here yesterday."

Blithely defending herself, ~~Andrea~~ *Kimberly* told me she had turned on the furnace; I was surprised, "I'll bet this time last year you would have sat here in the cold, freezing... Progress!"

"I was up half the night. Be nice," she cautioned in jest rolling her eyes.

"I couldn't sleep either," I said, hugging my wool coat around me. "Did you see the new billboard for Westbury Park?" I asked.

"Yeah. Why?"

"It says, 'Move *up* to Westbury'," I explained. Emphasizing *up*, I lifted one hand over the other.

Gasping, Andrea rummaged through a kitchen drawer, claiming the name of her house plan was *The Jefferson*, as in the old television show. She opened a green folder and laid the plan down pointing to the name in print; it was true.

"Tony and I used to joke and sing, 'we're movin' on up...' when we drove out here before we moved in," she confessed.

Amused with her admission, I sang the familiar sit-com jingle myself. Cutting it off before we took it too far, I managed a slightly more serious tone, saying, "Well, the billboard is a perfect example of what I've been thinking. Could there be a more deliberate way we try to seek temporary fulfillment, almost purposefully?" Answering my own question, I said, "If the intent of the advertisement is to appeal to the human need to rise up, be better than, or out perform, then it is a totally different distraction from gauzing."

Andrea poured my coffee saying, "We *are* all trying to get somewhere." We thought about how everyone is driving fast, walking fast, and crossing off their to-do lists.

In keeping with our jovial moods I said, "It reminds me of the amusement park ride, bumper cars. We jump into the coolest vehicle we can find and spend our day whirling around as fast as possible bumping into others and being bumped." I stirred the cream into my coffee watching it swirl around the mug as I said, "The entire time we have no real path or direction and then the game is over. We don't win or lose, yet we get in every time with the enthusiasm for victory."

Andrea

Despite our good-humored demeanor, the idea of thinking we were heading somewhere, yet going nowhere started growing more uncomfortable. We were again confronted with the sheer tendency in all of us to stay the course despite the route never resulting in a better outcome for our lives. There seemed to be obliviousness on all of our parts that Kimberly and I were identifying as separate from gauzing, yet equally programmed.

Kimberly

Trying to be as concise as I could, I told Andrea, "What if we apply the age old idea of being on a ladder?" She grimaced, not wanting to hear the rest as I persisted, "Try not to think of the corporate or social ladders; this is something different." The image of the ladder was clear to me as I continued, "I'm talking about the fleeting sense of comfort that comes from reaching for the next best thing, gaining upward momentum with each achievement, thinking we're getting ahead."

"Alright," Andrea said drawing up a chair. "Go on."

"People are out seeking a sense of status as if it were a destination. We try so hard at winning, being the best, or succeeding that at times it feels more about the position on the rungs than the journey it takes to get there." I stopped abruptly wondering if that was what I did when moving to Westbury Park. "Fighting to get to the top could be impeding our real happiness or meaningful lives because our focus is on what we think is the end result, the crescendo of our driven-ness."

The various ways we climb on and over one another paraded through my head. The mom, who makes sure to announce how many times she's taxied her kids to practice, steps up a rung, closer to the prize for busiest soccer mom. A name dropping socialite scales toward proving he is somebody because he is "up there" with the best. The man who spends countless extra hours working at his job in order to be considered the top in his field is elevating himself.

Our position, which felt visible to everyone, kept us struggling to somehow reach a better, more impressive rung. It meant everything in our lives held the possibility of providing the edge needed to assist in our ascent: newer car, bigger house, impressive degree, influential friends, Hollywood figure… each boosting our sense of rising closer to the ultimate prize. A promotion at work, winning an argument, noticing that second glance from someone… they all made us feel like we were movin' on up.

We were also overly concerned with who stood next to us on the rungs. If we looked to our right and left and felt comparable to those around us, our neighbors, club members, co-workers, and so on, we were more content than if we did not approve of who was nearby us on the ladder. It caused a sense of "less-than" if we noticed someone coming up and mingling among our peers, who was considered beneath us. We wanted to keep good company on the ascent.

Andrea

When Kimberly paused in thought, I added, "Keeping a tally system in relationships sets us on a ladder as well. Totaling up the score allows us to see who's getting ahead, and who is falling behind. It becomes exhausting trying to keep track so we can keep up all the time."

I thought of how often I'd listed my jobs out in my head or shouted them at Tony, "I took out the trash, and that's *your* job." More times than not, I actually felt as if others had climbed over me. Even when Tony did something nice for me it felt like he was moving past me to go for an award I wanted. If he did the dishes or threw in a load of laundry, I had to tell him he didn't do it right, "Now those shirts will fade, those forks shouldn't have been upside down…" I had to shove him back, away from out-doing me.

In exasperation, I asked, "Why does hanging on to the rung of 'I know more than you' or 'I've worked harder than you' somehow feel like a win?"

Without directly answering my question, Kimberly shook her head in agreement.

Kimberly

The ladder analogy showed why some people reacted with revenge, gossip, or passive aggression when they believed they weren't given credit, and someone else was. As we spoke, I could see little fights breaking out where people converged on the rungs. The shoving and pulling, also known as gossip and backstabbing, could become vicious when we felt someone overtook us. It made us think we were somehow being forced back or passed over. I told Andrea, "We're infused with the feeling, 'Others are getting what I want'." It also made sense of why we would go on to discount an accomplishment we secretly wanted, but thought we could never reach.

Andrea

Seemingly overcome by the obvious sense of endless effort, Kimberly sighed, "Climbing up the ladder is about excess and attainment, forcing our way past people, and striving to be the best despite who gets trampled. Standing on our successes and pointing out who has less is very egocentric as the drive is to get more, have more, and be more. We push ourselves up… to God, our boss, our spouse, ourselves."

"That's interesting, egocentric," I consented, "you're not really thinking about the other people. You're just thinking about how you can have more and how the successes of others make you look or feel." Then, I asked, "Can you think of *anyone* who is driven in this way, who thinks they have 'arrived' or have 'made it'?"

Kimberly

Flicking the red and white stirrer in my coffee cup I answered, "No, I can't." I grabbed the warm red mug with both hands and uttered, "What if that's because there was no lasting sense of reward for any of it? I mean what if you could pan back and look at the ladder from space to see the climb never ended? What if the ladder kept spiraling tall, soaring above the clouds until we were exhausted and hardly able to breathe, still hanging on for that glory, each effort always leaving us short of the crest wanting more?

What if we couldn't ever feel the accomplishment because there was no end to the ladder?"

I paused again, the room static from the scope of the comprehension. I knew the end to this analogy was not good as I said in shame, "In time, some people lose their grip, realizing the scope of the climb and its continual battle." We talked about the celebrities and the sports stars and the CEO's, the people who, by society's standards, had "made it." Yet many of those people struggled with meaning realizing the pinnacle was not a destination or accomplishment, but a perception they could never fully control. The strain of maintaining life on the ladder, or the realization that it was not real or meaningful was so difficult, that the thought of what could come next escaped my breath. We slumped in our chairs thinking the fall could fracture people's minds, break their hearts, or take their lives; we fell silent for a moment, both pausing in contemplation.

Andrea

In the quiet, it occurred to me, *As Christians we're supposed to be different from the "world" but we don't understand how, so we appraise the morality of people around us and make comparisons to build ourselves up.* Categorizing sins as big or little went against the *Bible* teaching that if you transgress on one point, you've broken the entire law; which somehow never felt quite fair. Yet, I considered how Christians would agree all sin is equal in the eyes of God, while still insisting certain behaviors marked people as clearly unsaved.

Interrupting the silence, I said, "Christians choose a list of things we are not generally tempted to do, like sleep with another person of our own gender and post it on the ladder as a moral compass reading, 'Don't fall below this rung'." Kimberly knew I had been guilty of saying things such as, "I don't drink and run around like that." We both saw how most of the Christians in the room could start feeling really safe when the subject of homosexuality came up, thinking, *I would never do that*, as they looked down on those they believed to be beneath them on the ladder.

Pondering the way I'd acted, I said, "We know we are not sinless; therefore, we categorize the sin to make ourselves feel closer to God." The sin categories were used as cardinal points on the compass. By pinpointing our direction we could convince ourselves we were safe as long as we avoided heading due south. As I concluded my thought, I imagined the faulty navigation tool guiding us in circles around the ladder, until we slipped and went plummeting down in a way we never saw coming, like the big named pastors and evangelists embezzling money or having affairs. In that way, religion presented elements of life on a spiritual ladder. We desperately try to rise up, clinging onto each other, fighting to elevate ourselves as much as we can. Having the illusion of getting closer to God when we condemn sins we don't commit, we're really just hurting others as we push them under ourselves. I confessed, "Thinking of Christians in this way gives me the impression that perhaps we, too, need to be saved."

"Perhaps?" Kimberly asked.

"Well," I acknowledged, "The *Bible* says there is a reward, but it's not at the top of anything, and it's not for being better than others."

Kimberly

Even if, as Christians, we knew enough to be free from trying to keep up with others, we were still driven within ourselves to reach an ever prominent aspiration. Setting goals and striving to meet them was not a bad concept; however, I saw how that grain of truth could pollute our lives like a cancer cell if it grew into a mindset of proving to ourselves, and the people around us, that we were becoming somebody. Just as gauze temporarily stopped the bleeding, ladder climbing kept people preoccupied with rank in a restless manner, as if their existence depended on attaining a number of status awards and in due course, reaching the pinnacle. Seeing the ladder for what it was, I felt pressed between something I knew and something I was coming to know.

Andrea

Cutting the strain, I suggested, "We need a break." The painter's white cargo van drove past my front window from the newly built house up the street, so I asked, "Want to go see the new house? The painter just left. If we don't get in there soon, the family is going to move in; we'll miss our chance." I threw my on coat and adjusted the scarf I was already wearing.

"Let's go!" Kimberly agreed, buttoning her coat and taking the last gulp of her coffee.

Within minutes we'd walked down the street and were trying the back door; it was unlocked. Inside, the floors and counters were gorgeous, and the appliances in the kitchen gave me a twinge of envy; they were some of the nicest I'd ever seen. We gave ourselves a tour, oohhing and ahhhing, pointing out things we could have or should have done in our own homes. As we were about to leave, we heard the engine of a car. Rushing to the window, we saw the family's gray minivan parking in the driveway. Tip toeing out of sight, we huddled at the front door. We were caught.

Panicked, I asked, "What's the etiquette on showing yourself through someone's house before they move in?" I hoped they would enter through the garage so we could slip out the front.

"There must be different rules for vacant properties," Kimberly answered sarcastically mimicking my concern, almost enjoying the tension.

Standing deer eyed to our new neighbors from inside their own front door, I spoke first, "Hi." I tilted my head politely folding my hands, "We live right up," I pointed the wrong way, "down the street...just coming in to see..."

"How nicely everything is done," Kimberly interrupted, suddenly using her radio personality voice. "It really is beautiful." Her guilty grin grew bigger solidifying into a smile.

I didn't realize I'd been holding my breath, until I sighed in relief as Mrs. New Owner told us she didn't care about our curiosity. She wanted to share her ideas about built-in shelves and storage solutions. Walking back into the kitchen, she directed our attention to her six-burner stove. By her third comment on her expertise in the kitchen, I was aggravated. *She doesn't know who she's talking to,* I thought, picturing my own six-burner stove.

Walking home, I was fuming. Hearing her talk about soufflés and quiches and double wall ovens, I thought, *She's not a chef; she didn't go to school for it. I can cook like a chef. All you need is a good recipe.* This bazaar feeling of irritation and a desire to outcook her was pressing in on me, but before I started to make derogatory comments to Kimberly about our new neighbor; I thought about the ladder. I was ready to put down the woman I'd just met because I feared she was trying to shove me off the rung of best cook, which I had been clinging to for years. But as an alternative, I admitted to Kimberly how I was feeling.

"You know," I said, "This is the first time I resisted the urge to say something mean about another person and tell the truth about what was really motivating the remarks I wanted to make." I realized it was probably what the *Bible* meant when it admonished us to confess our faults one to another. I added, "I guess you could say I'm aware of the temptation of living on that never ending ladder." I relaxed into the realization that nothing was being claimed, no prize was at stake. Instead of thinking of the woman as competing with me, I could think about how fun it was going to be to learn more about her.

Kimberly

I had to admit, Ed and I, as a couple, had been climbing the ladder for as long as we'd known each other. I'd been on it my whole life. We both thought the prize at the top was utopia, I guess, because we worked hard to achieve. I was climbing as a young girl trying to become good enough to study dance in New York. I then had to finish my BA in less than four years and own my first home by the time I was twenty five. I had to switch from one job to another to keep rising. I left social work to go into administration, leaving that for the corporate world. I attained the top corporate position in my field with the expense account and company car to match. Ed did the same thing with the same results.

Each move or job change had us thinking this was "it!" I had no idea what "it" was, though. We never discussed it. We were too tired from all the effort of the climb. We could never celebrate our moments along way, because if we could move up just a little more, then we'd be successful and happy. That *if-then* scenario had played out for 13 years in our marriage. Looking very upper middle class, very successful, had made us no different. We just saw higher rungs waiting to be climbed.

The discussion of the day had again proven the human tendency to react and respond in reflex rather than thoughtful self-reflective awareness. With Andrea, who thought about climbing over another woman due to her cooking skills, and Ed and I stressing ourselves to reach "the top," the ladder climber analogy became a grotesque look into more programmed responses. They were evidence of the unconscious reactions that kept us hanging on to it everyday. *Could we strive to be the best without needing to be the best? Could we achieve success and see it as something we do, something to enhance our lives, without seeing it as who we are?* Why was that making more sense than it ever had before?

Chapter 9

Carnival Cut-outs: Pinching the Gorilla's Nipple

Andrea

Thanksgiving had always been my family's most anticipated holiday, with piles of delicious food and a day fully devoted to devouring all of it. We had hosted the holiday meal for my extended family, and after cleaning up all weekend, I was preparing to spend Monday decorating for Christmas.

Kimberly stopped by with a box of doughnuts, and two cups of steaming hot coffee from the drive-through. Stepping over the totes full of bulbs and garland I had spread out everywhere, she cocked her head to the side asking, "You decorate without your kids?"

"I don't want them messing it up," I defended.

"Merry Christmas," she teased sarcastically, handing

me a cream stick.

"They *do* have a separate little tree," I explained. "They cover it with golden macaroni ornaments, paper lanterns, and photographs, whatever they've made over the years. They get to boss their own tree."

Sitting down on the couch with two coffees and enough sugar to keep it interesting, I knew I wouldn't be accomplishing much in preparation for the holidays.

Kimberly

"Well Thanksgiving was... unusual," I said, taking a bite. "All I can say is my family thinks I 'drank the Kool-aid' for sure now."

"What did you do?" Andrea wondered, implying my fault. She knew me too well.

"I just showed them one Jesus video! Just one," I smirked, taking another bite.

"Shut up!"

"Remember the video Brent showed during his sermon a few weeks ago?" I asked. "The one about when the rain falls in our lives to remember we have a Father who will shelter us from the storm...the tear jerker?"

"Stop," Andrea held her hand out as if to halt me. "No you didn't..."

"I did. I thought it could help my sister, you know, to deal with anxiety...stress," I started laughing. "It was an eleven minute video. How bad could it have been?"

Trying to conceal amusement, she asked, "Was it well received?"

"Pretty much what I expected; my parents tried to smile through it but said very little. My sister seemed at first to view it as a joke but then became defensive. My brother walked out of the room before it started." Knowing how absurd I must have seemed, I laughed harder, "They think I'm nuts!"

Andrea was laughing with me, "That's the last movie they will ever let you pick." She hugged her side, "Forget decorating for Christmas, they're gonna skip coming to your house."

"Well, I'll send them a Jesus e-mail, then; I don't care." I played along, knowing I would never. "They're just unsure of how to take me now that I'm showing inspirational videos and claiming to have found God in my life. They're not used to me saying stuff like that."

Andrea

"I hear you on that one. My family is so accustomed to me being a certain way, that breaking out of the pattern sets off mini explosions all around me. Everyone is used to me trying to hold it all together. I love my family so much, but I've worked hard to make a perfect life, or at least appear to have a perfect life."

Kimberly raised her eye brows questioning my admission without a word, letting me go on. "For so long, I've lived what my sister refers to as 'the life of the white sheet'. I was terrified something was going to stain my sheet or mark it. I lived pacing around it or falling asleep on the sheet, fearing the threat of something sullying it or affecting me and my family." I explained how every person, place, and thing was evaluated as safe to touch the sheet or having potential to mess it up. I admitted, "What people think of me feels paramount to how I view myself. I always wonder, 'What will people think? What will they say?' I've always been concerned about trying to seem Christ-like."

Kimberly asked, "So now you're not as worried about

those things?"

"I am... a little, but not like I used to be. It's just that everybody still sees me the way I thought I wanted them too. I've been thinking about the roles I've found myself in, as if they represent an exterior depiction of me." I waved my hand around as if to clear the thought but continued explaining, "Think of a row of life-sized cut-outs: one of me as a mother, one as a Republican, a wife... a Christian."

"Oh!" Kimberly said throwing up her hands, "like the painted wooden boards you stand behind for pictures. I have one of those pictures with Ed. He's behind a muscle bound gorilla man. I'm next to him, behind a sexy bikini clad seductress who is leaning in pinching his nipple." She snickered, adding, "It's from our honeymoon." She described exactly what I meant, carnival cut-outs.

Knowing the idea of masking ourselves or being artificial, I was expressing one final way I saw people reacting without thinking. I would never have considered myself to be fake or insincere but facing myself, I realized, "Though I was never really conscious of thinking, *I want people to think of me this way*, I kept stepping up to an image of a wife...then behind the image of a mom... then a Christian. The entire time poking my head through, I smiled, being the face of whatever image I felt expected to be. I was trying to live up to the ideal."

We talked about the embarrassing and gullible ways we ran from behind one image to another. We both had our images of choice, from daughter, to popular high school girl, dancer, college student, girlfriend, and on to wife and mother, room mother. The cut-outs were there, and the people in my life continued coming, expecting me to pop my head through, not interested in who I was behind the board of impressions. I wanted to please the audience so I smiled.

"Did I ever tell you about the teas we served at the Father's House?" I asked.

Shaking her head no, Kimberly curled her feet up under herself on the sofa and sank into the cushions knowing I was about to tell a story.

"My mom, sister, and I were in charge of 'The Tea' at the cult-church's house of ministry. My aunt, who was our leader, had people come to the house to spend the night. She would pray to set them free from 'spiritual bondage'." I went on explaining how we served extravagant tea-style brunches to groups of women every other weekend for about five years. The menu was always beautifully printed, and we only served on the finest china. We had the tea down to a perfect art. We shopped and chopped the day before and baked the morning of. Everything had to be fresh; after all, it was for God.

The thick aromas of both sweet and savory delicacies wafted through the Victorian style, century home owned by the church. As Nora ministered, the kitchen filled with tangy citrus scents from the lemons we sliced and studded with cloves. The dining room warmed with the awareness of freshly baked breads topped with rich pâtés and slices of roasted meat or seafood. Each weekend the tea had its own new, fresh floral arrangement. Some were to the ceiling and mingled with ribbons, others had fish swimming in their vases, but almost all had vines which cascaded over the edges of the table.

In white gloves and hand-sewn aprons, we smiled and served giving the impression it was *nothing* to display such a sumptuous spread. We impressed every lady who came to have her demons cast out. I was respected and reliable, but I had to do more and more to feel close to God, while my circle of friends was shrinking to exclude even my favorite people. I never thought of it as being an image. I always tried to be the best I could be, but by allowing existing ideas to dictate what the best was, I had lived into an image.

Kimberly

"There was nothing unwise in trying to excel or be the best, but I think the problem came in when you became more about the approval than the mastering of the task," I said trying to make the distinction between the ladder and carnival cut-outs. "On the ladder, it's about wanting to get to the top to attain some sense of status. As a cut-out, it's all about affirmation; trying to please others' expectations of what's best." I flashed back to my own need to be affirmed by my father.

Agreeing, Andrea quietly added, "I knew what people wanted, and I gave it to them."

Andrea

As a housewife, the façade was trying to live in a spotlessly clean home and unruffled life. Although my family had cooperated and the house was clean, I still wasn't happy. I was consumed with aggravation over the inevitable undoing of all my hard work. Like a temple worker serving the image of perfection, I must have believed if I made plentiful sacrifices, the god of Clean House would rain down blessings of happiness and fulfillment. I was faithful to my image, rarely coming out from behind it, but the blessings never came. I was lonely behind that wooden board, and tired of lugging it with me all day, everyday. The home supposed to serve me as a shelter became my master.

Often, when I walked through the door in the evening to a messy house after working all weekend for the church, I'd stumble under the weight of both cut-outs, tripping and falling onto the images. I'd run out of energy in the privacy of my home, inevitably revealing the beleaguered, frightened woman I fought so hard to hide. Yelling and screaming about the house, which I felt reflected on me, I would explode in anger on my husband and children. Ranting and crying until I could pull myself together I'd scramble back behind my façade. From the front of the board, I was a mature, apron clad Christian, smiling next to a nice house, a nice husband, and well behaved kids. From the back of the board, I was shaking from fatigue trying to keep it from crashing down around me. I would repent for becoming upset and promise to be more organized and patient. I'd plan on doing better at holding it in the next time I felt overwhelmed.

Kimberly

I spent the rest of the day thinking about the façades in my life. I wondered, taking a chilly, winter walk alone through my neighborhood, how many cut-outs lived on our street. The national statistics for marriages ending in divorce were over 50%, yet we all got together often with casserole dishes and happy faces. It would be nice to be real enough to really know people and share in their lives, but living out from behind the boards would be exposing and frightening. *People must think it's easier to carry on in the pain of a façade,* I decided as a set of Christmas lights came to life with the gently turning heads of white ornamental deer. I asked myself, *Is that what I believe?*

At times, I smiled when I wanted to cry, or hid behind

the "I can do it all" cut-out, which left me resentful toward Ed when he didn't help. I presented myself in a way that I thought people wanted, and I tried to make sure everyone was happy even if it meant I was lying. I couldn't deny the cut-outs were inaccurate portrayals of who I was. Yet I rushed to stand behind each wooden depiction. Waiting for the image to be preserved, as if with the snap of a flash bulb, I'd forever be seen the way I wanted.

Instead, I found myself carrying their weight around wherever I went, pulling them out one-by-one depending upon those around me, and what they wanted, what they expected. I was the "creative mom," the "witty niece," the "career woman." Very few people ever saw the real woman behind the board, and as my life funneled down, I didn't even recognize myself. I hoped for real relationships, wanted to show and give real love, but when presented with the opportunity, I pulled out a familiar cut-out and pushed my head through. It was so predictable to others and even to myself that those personas became "who" I was. I had convinced everyone, including myself at some point. Believing my own propaganda, I became unable to come to any perspectives about my unfulfilling life... until now.

Andrea

My very morality had been a thinly veiled show. When I was around other people, I felt I had to be the good Christian. My favors and jobs or ministries were done with great effort, while I acted as if it all came with ease. At the time, I thought I was illustrating the power of God to enable me to excel, being a good example without complaining. I never wanted to let somebody see incapability or weakness in me, so I hid behind the depiction of a saint, trying to be presentable for God. I was in fear of God's anger toward how I looked to other people and in fear of His judgment on my choices. I hid myself away in an effort to become my idea of a Christian and to avoid making any decisions at all. This seemed to be what Jesus meant when He told the parable of the wicked servant, who fearing his master, buried his talent instead of investing it or even just putting it in the bank.

Kimberly

The days passed quickly as the world bustled along readying itself for Christmas. I pulled out the nativity set Ed's grandmother had given to us years before, the one for which I never seemed to find a place. I set it up in the kitchen on a small table to remind myself Jesus didn't come into the world to help me protect my image. Feeling oddly comfortable with the collection of figurines, I headed out to Andrea's house. We were meeting with a pastor's wife from another church. Andrea had met her at a soccer tournament, in the fall, where they'd had a few conversations about their spirituality. After bumping into her at the store, Andrea invited her to take a break from the crazy holiday pace and join us for coffee the following morning. I was looking forward to meeting her.

I noticed, sitting around the new table in Andrea's dining room, we were all smiley. It made me laugh with the awareness of how far I'd come in my beliefs. The pastor's wife, Jan, began to take the conversation to an unexpected place. She said quietly, "You both," looking at Andrea and then me, "have no idea how difficult it is to try and fit into the role of a pastor's wife when your wishes take you elsewhere."

Sitting there shocked, Andrea replied, "I often wondered

about that. Do you ever just want to be...yourself?"

Jan was trying to hold back tears, but they began flowing uncontrollably. She had to let it out. "I love my church, my husband, the people in the church," she said, dobbing the corners of her eyes, "but I want to go back to school, I want to work in the real world... full time. I want to sit in the back of church on Sundays and I want to wear jeans." She stopped and looked up aware of her admission. Andrea and I were taken aback by her openness. We had been discussing the façades in our lives all week, and her story was so similar to ours.

We talked for hours about the roles women find themselves being funneled into. Noticing she was going to be late to pick her daughter up from school, she excused herself. Hugging us, she said warmly, "It was so refreshing being here today, with you girls. Let's do this again...soon." We agreed and mentioned how we'd be seeing her at an upcoming event at Old North Church. When she left, Andrea and I were struck by the glimpse we had of such a beautiful woman from behind the cut-out. I related in sadness, "She is really just a person trying to do her best, caught in a world she's not sure would allow her the safety of sharing herself."

Andrea

On the evening of the women's Advent dinner at Old North church, the sky was black but clear and dotted with beautiful white stars. The cool air carried huge white snow flakes and the smell of wood burning from nearby chimneys; I couldn't remember a more festive moment. Kimberly and I were ready to dress up and head out for a girls' night on the town. It had been a long week, and we were up for some fun.

I picked her up and complimented her blouse, which resembled the New Years Eve ball that drops annually in Times Square. She was proud of the sparkles and made sure to ask if I noticed how her lotion and eye makeup sparkled too. I was feeling especially young and fashionable as well, as I had gone to a fancy store in Cleveland where my sister worked to buy a new big city outfit. I had come a long way from ankle length dresses and aprons with matching white gloves, but it didn't occur to me we might be over-dressed until we rolled into the parking lot and noticed *every* other woman was wearing black pants.

Kimberly pulled the invitation out of her sequined clutch and flipped it over and then back.

"Is there a dress code?" She asked.

I looked at the ladies streaming through the parking lot, who appeared to be in uniform. We saw Jan step out of her car and smooth the pleats of her black wool slacks. I reached for the invitation; I had to read it myself.

"Dear God, we are the only two people who aren't wearing black pants," I shouted, backing into a parking space so we could observe the parking lot parade; we hoped at least one other person would be as enthusiastically clothed.

Kimberly pointed and made an odd sound, a burst of laughter through her nose, "There…" I turned to see a young mom who wasn't wearing black pants. My hope circling the drain, as I saw she had on a long skirt; it was black.

"I can't walk in there. I'm wearing fishnet hose," I yelled, not sure I thought it was funny.

Kimberly was slapping her leg and completely cracking up, she was pointing to my shoes. All she could manage to say between laughing and trying to breathe was, "They're red. Red, shoes."

I was starting to sweat. Looking down at myself, I finally laughed too, "Well, I guess if I would have been thinking about fitting in..." I snapped my hose back against my leg. We knew after all of our talk about being an image, going home to change would have been a step backwards. We realized being ourselves wasn't always as comfortable as we would have hoped. There was enough sameness in the world to make us want to hide some of ourselves away, or at least be embarrassed if we weren't because no one wants to feel odd.

Kimberly composed herself, wiping the smeared mascara from under her eyes, "We have to go in. Strong, well dressed, Christian women don't hide behind the cut-outs."

As we walked in, quickly to our table of course, I click clacked along in my strapy, red high heals with nude colored fishnets under a torn organdy ruffle on my pink skirt. Kimberly was beside me wearing a disco ball blouse reflecting light off of her sparkly skin. As we tucked ourselves into our seats, we nodded in the direction of one of the few other soul sisters who'd dressed up in fancy array.

Chapter 10

The Bronze Statue: A Bubble In the Forehead

Kimberly

What happened in our new approach to sin was it related way more to my life than I expected. I honored my mother and father, I did not kill, or commit adultery, or covet thy neighbors *anything*. How was it now, sinning for me included the subtle ones, the sins that may not be so obvious yet were just as damaging? Gauzing, climbing, and the cut-outs, were new ideas to me. They were all relevant to my life, relevant to everyone. I learned I couldn't make myself feel better by damaging my body or make my life better by making someone else's worse, and I certainly couldn't live my life from behind an image. I wanted to stop, so did Andrea. We were ready to change.

Andrea

I thought of something, and I couldn't wait to talk about it. I knew the true definition of sin was to miss the mark so as to not obtain the prize, so the questions then became; what is the mark? What is the prize?

It was a little early in the morning, but I called Kimberly, who listened as I explained, "The mark is pleasing God. The prize is going to heaven. Though in that regard, Christianity is reduced. It's reduced to a practice of performing then waiting for paradise." I had spent determined hours diligently trying to please God, doing what I thought was best; but it didn't matter because I was left wondering, *What else does He want from me?* I never felt that I had really done enough. This also failed to make sense given my understanding that a person couldn't earn her way into Heaven, so I tried looking at it a different way.

I theorized, "Say the mark is friendship, because it is the goal, the thing you want. You 'fire the arrow' of gossip just to get a conversation going or to have something interesting to say. Even if there is a short-term payoff, gossip is something that will never result in true friendship, so you do not obtain the prize." It easily translated out into other things as well. I gave a second example, "A woman wants to feel loved and wanted so she 'fires the arrow' of looking as pretty as she can and giving her body to whoever makes her feel special. She wanted love, but she feels used and so clearly missed the mark she was going for."

"It works, but it feels too small," Kimberly interjected. "From a psychology standpoint it begs the question, why do people have these needs in the first place, needs which drive them to do anything to get what they feel is missing?"

Kimberly

We knew it was God who was missing, but since we had identified the tendency to turn faith into a survival of the fittest, the fact remained: believing in Jesus, reading a *Bible*, not drinking or having the "bad kind of sex" was still not enough to keep us from the drive to sin. *What else is there*, we wondered.

Andrea listened as I considered, "If the woman in the scenario knows she wants love, but fishes for it with sex; she's likely to end up with a man who will use her, not what she hoped for. If someone wants a friend but spends her time gossiping and putting other women down as a way to 'connect,' she shouldn't be surprised when she finds herself attracting 'friends' who enjoy gossip enough to stab *her* in the back one day. A husband may believe what he wants is a happy wife and home, but he fires the arrow of control and criticism trying to hit the target. It may be subconscious, but that happens every day."

I knew the people in our examples may not be aware of what they really wanted or of what they were settling for instead. I thought about the concept admitting, "It takes vulnerability to step out and admit what you really want and how you really feel, and more than that, to have a clear understanding of what underscores every desire we have as humans, which is to be loved and valued." I thought of our promise and how we had to be honest to have a real friendship, setting aside the images we wanted to be associated with and the scenarios of ladder climbing and gauzing usually found in friendships.

We ended our early morning phone call with a plan to meet at Andrea's for lunch after finishing a few chores and morning errands.

Andrea

Kimberly walked up my driveway for lunch just as the UPS truck pulled in. She met the driver as he jumped down with his electronic clip board. I watched, guessing Tony was expecting another delivery of promotional items for work, a box of logo pens or tire gauges. She tried to take the huge box from the driver, but it was too large and awkward for her to carry. The thought occurred to me, *Those aren't pens.*

Signing the slip, I leaned in to see where the package originated from, hoping for a clue to its contents.

"Open it!" Kimberly insisted.

When packages came to my house, they were rarely for me; this was an exception. The label read, Elements of Home, with an Illinois mailing address. I pulled back the tape exposing the air-filled plastic bags cushioning the concealed item.

"What the heck?" Kimberly squinted trying to guess, watching me unwrap.

"It's… Ummm… A statue?" I said stunned. Lifting the eighteen inch bust of a Greek athlete from the shipping box, I realized, "My mother told me that she'd ordered something for me, but that was so long ago that I forgot. I certainly wasn't expecting a statue."

Kneeling on the floor in the foyer, I looked up into Tony's office, wanting to place it perfectly. Once settled in the corner of the room, angled toward the front door as if to welcome guests, it was an absolute wonder; I loved it. Kimberly sat on the office bench and I spun in Tony's desk chair to admire my new gift. The sculpture resembled an archeological find, as if weathered and a little worn from the daunting task of surviving centuries of ware; that was part of what made it look so authentic.

Interrupting the quiet, I offered, "A few years ago my mom took an art class with me from a man who made molds and then used them to cast statues of bronze. He spent countless hours preparing each mold to be exactly what he wanted and then had the bronze slowly poured into each one to complete his design."

"I'm sure his work was beautiful," Kimberly answered.

"It was; each piece was its own masterpiece when finished." I leaned in and brushed away some flecks of cardboard from the statue. *How much work must have gone into creating this athlete?* I wondered. Thinking about God as the Creator, myself as His masterpiece, I asked, "What if the mold could decide for itself to form a giant bubble leaving a void in the bronze?" Knowing it sounded a bit odd at first, I continued, "Or if it could decide to pull other things into itself, trying to fill up faster, as the artist slowly poured the bronze?" It made me wonder if the statue would be an accurate reflection of what the artist had intended to make, what he was capable of making. "With the mold removed to expose the finished statue, if there were a bubble on the forehead or a gap in the neck, or if a foreign object was sticking out of the cheek bone, would the results be less than the artist had planned?" Rolling the chair around, I faced my friend.

"Of course," she answered, making the connection, "If people are the magnificent work of God's hands, like a statue being poured slowly over time, then we must ask ourselves if we are a true result of what we were designed to become."

Kimberly

We sat silently, and I could sense the explanation of the flawed bronze statue. It was an example of the end result of hours spent gauzing, ladder climbing, and hiding behind an image, pulling things into and around ourselves that were not part of God's plan for our lives. The constant struggle left us falling further and further away from our intended selves. We concluded sin in whatever form was offensive to God because it caused His magnificent creation to become less than He'd intended. If every time we chose against becoming His masterpiece, we were altering not only who we were created to be, but the work of the artist; it was as costly to the Creator as it was to the creation.

We wondered if a cloud of witnesses was leaning over the edge of heaven breathlessly waiting and wondering, "Who will this one be? What will she look like? What makes her stand out?" We decided we would want to accurately depict the intent of the Artist. Placed effectively where we could reflect His work, we wanted to find a way to be who God intended.

I immediately thought of myself when, as a young college student, I had come to the place of choosing which path to take toward the future. I had wanted so desperately to take the riskier opportunity, which lead back to New York to pursue my dream versus the alternative, a safer option leading to marriage and an acceptable career. I was not pushed or coerced; it was my decision, and I chose safety. My safe life had since afforded the advantages of living close to family, having a good husband, four wonderful children, and a great career. However, I was realizing, in going against what makes me who I am, I became almost unrecognizable, even to myself.

It stirred uneasiness inside my soul, an uneasiness

that I tried to calm by soothing in seemingly harmless and sometimes damaging ways. Often, I ignored the uneasiness, but that squelching caused it to bubble out as anxiety and internal turmoil. My soul knew what my mind would not accept. I had reshaped my own life, away from God, and my design left me gaping and empty and lost. I had fallen short of the glory of God.

Andrea

I saw myself as an example too. When I dropped out of school refusing to show my potential, I caused a void in the bronze. I could blame my aunt, who certainly deserved some fault, but the loss was of something greater than my education or even my future. Feeling the sadness, I admitted, "I was lost; the only one who could ever be me struggled in a tiny life I'd made for myself when there was a huge world I refused to join. I became a product of my fears and anger, hurts and choices instead of developing into who God had planned."

Kimberly

"What happens?" I asked, focusing on the lives so many people stay huddled in. "I mean, as children we live with abandon, but we grow into adulthood and lose ourselves. The child in us, who would once dance in the rain, smell the flowers, or let the puppy lick her face fades away." I considered the number of people poking their heads through the cut-outs giving up the lead role in their existences or the people distracted, numb and gauzing, or climbing against God's plan for their lives. Somewhere in our childhoods, we modified ourselves to fit into an expectation, instead of living out our intended lives. *Was it a choice? Were we forced? Were we even aware of the shift?*

Andrea

This seemed to be the aspect of becoming childlike which Jesus referred to saying, unless we changed and became like little children, we would never enter the Kingdom of Heaven. The thing is, a little child doesn't think about the mess. A child looks at a puppy and sees a little ball of fluff. That's how I had been when younger, loving animals, bringing home stray and injured creatures. Nursing them to health, I'd gladly love and hold them, thinking I'd grow up to have a house full one day. Instead, I married a man who didn't want to bother with the mess of pets, so *we* weren't dog people. We weren't cat people or hamster people either. Our home was a pet free society, where Tony became encompassing as I remained invisible.

I'd made so much progress, taking time for myself to visit and hang out with Kimberly. Tony was becoming friends with Ed, and engaging in activities he would once have fought against. I could sense though, as I detached further from my cut-out, I didn't know who I was. Who even knew if I still loved animals or if I wanted to go certain places or do different things? I became aware, I was who Tony thought I was, or should be, an extension of my husband. I'd molded myself to fit into *his* life.

Somehow, a day came and without noticing, I transferred from oblivious living to cautious calculating. There were maturity issues and smart living decisions which should accompany growing up, but I had become enshrouded by others, eclipsed. In trying to please people, I whittled away extra activities and things I was passionate about. It was a paring down, which resulted in being less than God intended.

In a flash, I saw myself eight years earlier, alone in

a hospital bed. I'd been in a slow steady labor for three days, and I had a raging infection, yet I allowed my quiet requests for help to be ignored. My cervix was tied tightly closed with what looked like a shoelace. My doctor insisted I was just being dramatic, though I had not complained or protested beyond calmly repeating I believed I was progressing in labor.

Shaking in agony, I laid gasping as the neonatolagist announced his refusal to become involved, shouting, "Her own doctor can figure out this mess! I'm not touching it!" He blasted a huff to the nurse, who shrugged as she turned off the light, and followed him into the hall. There in the dark, my tiny 21 week old son, Noah, was born onto the bloody bed. Exhaling with a surprisingly shrill scream, I waited hoping by some miracle he would move under the globs of matter surrounding his unresponsive body. The tie never gave way so my cervix tore away from my uterus. His skull was crushed as he ripped through, killing him. His death killed me a little bit too.

My aunt called the hospital, and I listened while she reminded me how King David's baby died, and he washed his face and ate. Denying the hurt was so much harder than it had ever been. I was trying to be strong, a good Christian, mature enough to endure through my son's death the way King David did. Lying awake that night in the hospital listening to the cries of the *living* new born babies I swallowed back tears. Gathering the strength of every emotion I'd ever starved of, I forced the pain down as far as I could sink it, then I sang into the darkness, "What a merciful, merciful, merciful God You are." I was convincing myself He was because I needed Him to be. I needed His mercy to help me stop feeling, so I lifted my voice and repeated those words until I slipped away in exhaustion.

Kimberly listened quietly, but whispered, "How much of yourself did you give away?"

"Being objective about how I lived my life is possible with the image of the bronze statue in mind," I admitted in shame and gratitude, seeing how the hours I spent writhing around in pain, silently losing my unborn child were bubbles in the bronze. Refusing to participate in my own decisions, allowing another person to tell me what to think or how to feel, was how I escaped from my own life. I shut myself off mentally and emotionally over and over, fearing responsibility for choices I could have made for myself, by myself.

Kimberly

"This is really heartbreaking," I said, recognizing we clearly had just come to some overwhelming concepts about our lives. "I knew we hurt, and have been hurt in the past, but this level of soul searching is not for the faint of heart," I gestured in comfort.

Andrea nodded, "That's why no one does it. It's too painful...looking at yourself this honestly."

I knew we were not finished. I paused, just to collect my thoughts, "So now what? How do we fix this?"

"What?" she asked, still in thought.

"If we're all broken, we would not be forsaken to muddle on through the mess, would we? There is an answer...there's got to be," I stood reaching to hug her, before leaving.

Andrea

Kimberly and I had long talks in the following days about recognizing sin in our own lives. I could finally see how one sin was equal to all the others in God's eyes. Becoming who God intended was the goal and sin was missing that mark. It left us stuffed with things God never wanted for us or found us empty where we should have been full. *But, why did Jesus say we are guilty of sin when we just think of it in our hearts?* My limited comprehension of God still made Him seem unreasonable and impossible to please.

Kimberly and I had three vivid examples of what people do and an analogy of why it was wrong, but we needed to know why we did it. We were close to the truth; we could feel it. We decided to present our own working definitions of sin, knowing they would help guide us into the understanding we needed. I wrote mine on a note card and asked Kimberly to do the same, thinking she would have a very similar definition. Interestingly, my definition of sin was about self. I totally centered the idea of sin on what I thought and how I was feeling, thinking, and doing. It was about self, I couldn't deny it.

- Anything we do to try to obtain pleasure, comfort, closeness, position, power or satisfaction -- physically, emotionally or spiritually -- that has already been condemned by God as incapable of providing.

  Kimberly

- Any thought, action, or emotion bringing us short of the glory of God.

That was my definition. I thought it was interesting in

that it was all about God. Life was about God, not me; I somehow finally understood that. I began to see *sin* as a disregard of the value that God had placed on me. I started to realize that it was not as much the specific sin itself but, rather, the cause of the sin was what was separating who I was from whom I was created to be. God was looking for all of us to become something wonderful and great and sin was impeding that potential. "It is a road block to our own divine destiny. But why? Why would someone block their potential given to them by God? Why would I?" I asked.

Andrea

I'd always thought of the glory of God as a hierarchy, as if God's glory streamed from Heaven to Earth and back, and we had failed at being as glorious as He. Over and over, I'd heard how wicked and evil I was; I would never measure up, never be good enough. Yet, I was always supposed to try. *Would God command me to keep blindly firing arrows knowing I'd never come close enough? Would He wait and watch while I flailed helplessly trying to be as glorious as He with no hope of ever being so, in this life or the next?* That no longer made sense to me.

This line of thinking would imply Adam and Eve were as glorious as God then, prior to committing the first sin, which could certainly never be the case. God is the Creator of the universe, the I Am. Men could never be equal in glory to God; therefore, falling short of His glory meant something else. If it was becoming the flawed bronze statue or less than intended, it wasn't that we were less glorious than God but that we were less than glorifying to Him. We had all come up short of what He had purposed, deviating from His hope for us; we had all used people and things in ways not intended, but how could we stop?

I had tried so hard to emulate the Jesus I'd been taught to follow. I thought I could shine as brightly as I could on God and Godly things, working and serving in the church. I had forced a "perfect" response whenever I could to try to be as glorifying to God as I could be, yet I lived every day knowing I was just lucky He was good enough to take pity on such a hideous and awful sinner. Trying to please God had exhausted me, and now I was realizing it had all made me even less worthy. We were about to learn what was lost, if not our equality with God's glory, if not our ability to live up to Him.

Chapter 11

Jesus:
The Death Which
Proves Our Worth

Andrea

Our daughters were taking a dance class together, so Kimberly and I waited for them every week in a dumpy little diner, in a nearby plaza. The greasy smells of fried chicken and hash browns greeted us at the door with the jingle of an old brass bell. Our server glanced over as we seated ourselves near the smudgy window. She rolled her eyes and wiped her hand on her stained apron. After taking our order for two coffees, she disappeared behind a swinging door. Re-emerging from the kitchen, she plopped two half-empty mugs of charred dark coffee in the middle of our table.

"That's the last of it," she declared.

Kimberly leaned forward, tipping the mug slightly as

she peeked down at the offering. "I've never been served half of a cup of coffee before," she giggled in a low whisper, as the waitress spun back toward the kitchen.

"I've always wanted to open my own coffee shop," I admitted, sliding my cup away from me. "I would call it Common Grounds. It would be a place to sit and talk, a place to find commonality."

Kimberly replied, "Would you be serving that?" She pointed to the fly flopped over on its back, legs curled up like tiny sticks.

I brushed it off the table and changed the subject, "Anyway, I've been wondering about the first Biblical record of human sin. Can we identify how that singular act possibly relates to people today?" Without waiting for a response, I launched into the garden story, "So a man and a woman started life with a perfect freedom and peace, a life filled with light and love. But…a lie was whispered to them; 'there is more'." There, with burnt beverages, in a sticky booth, the thoughts of our recent analogies filled my mind like the pieces of a puzzle. Those pieces began realigning to reveal the apple we were fed.

Kimberly

There is more, that thought sent an electrical shock right through me. I sat straight up, saying, "Think about what was believed. Eve believed she had to be as good as the best thing -- essentially, she heard, 'you're not enough the way you are, and this…',", pausing, I extended my arm, pretending to hold out the apple, "…'this will make you better.' Eve took the bait. She bit the apple."

Andrea

Sitting there with Kimberly, I felt the perspective focus in my mind. "If the reason behind taking the forbidden fruit was, 'I'm not good enough the way I am, and this will make me better,' then Eve believed a lie. It has always been a lie. All of these generations later, we shine the spotlight on her taking the fruit, going against the command of God, but we're still thinking 'I am not enough.' We're still being deceived." I knew if the lie was still in place the motivation to sin was there with it. I'd been fighting the sins, which were the symptoms of the disease, instead of fighting the disease of worthlessness itself. By applying Christian principles to a broken life I was struggling to heal up separate areas where the signs of brokenness became visible, rather than going to the heart of what was causing those behaviors.

Kimberly

The original sin was committed in immediate response to believing the lie of "not enough." Eve believed she had to do more, be more, have more; but why? Had Eve evaluated herself the way God did, complete and beautifully created, needing no enhancement, she would have walked away.

What was fundamentally lost in the fall was spiritual identity, who we were alone in front of God. Once Adam and Eve believed the lie of, "not good enough," they adopted the actions of an autonomous selfhood and acted upon that lie, the same lie we live today in our daily lives trying to find fulfillment. The deception was thinking something would make us better, the apple we are fed. We were still taking bites.

Andrea

I knew saying Eve took the bait not just out of pride, but also out of her need to be better, was an extension of the familiar understanding of original sin. This consideration went past what she did and explained why she did it. Sharing this could strike a nerve with seasoned Christians who liked to believe they had Jesus wrapped up and tied with a bow. Kim sat looking at me in shock, as I said something very direct. "If the traditional explanation of the garden story is complete the way I'd always understood it, then it should be applicable in our lives. It should be relatable, and yet it's not." Kimberly sat up and leaned forward nodding her head. I finished my thought, "Ask yourself this, are we walking around today wanting the knowledge of good and evil just as we were taught Eve desired? Do we all want wisdom; do we all want to be like God?"

Kimberly

I could feel the hairs standing up on the back of my neck. "No," I whispered intently trying to keep my excitement contained in such a public place. "People are trying to find a way to feel better," I said. Twirling around my mug to grab at the handle, I lifted it saying, "They are thinking, *this will make me better.*" People were trying to feel fulfilled. The pride was there in the decision to choose for one's self, but a powerful persuasion paved the way to that disobedience. The choice to act on the temptation was made because a lie was believed. Eve needed to be better and more pleasing to God because she thought she wasn't enough.

"Exactly," Andrea answered, "and that can be applied as the motivation behind so many Biblical stories and stories of people in our lives today." We listed, and shared random examples: Biblical Kings, former managers we'd worked under, school girls from junior high, an alcoholic relative, and the depressed, but smiling home-room mom who stayed up all night to make 20 dozen gingerbread cookies the kids all ate in under one minute. The lie permeated every aspect of our lives, blinding us to our worth, so we were left with the desperation of self-seeking behaviors to manufacture some sense of value.

We reflected on how even Eve herself was impacted. She set off a chain of events perpetuating the human need to find fulfillment, and was so ashamed after taking the fruit. *How often had I felt the same?* I knew it must be pride to think I could have what I want, when or how I want it, but pride does not usually result in shame. In fact, if it was just pride, Eve probably would have bragged about her choice. Instead, I think we are self-conscious because we've turned to things we instinctively know are wrong or not good for us. When we fail to realize our automatic responses come from a deeper need for worth, we are vulnerable to taking the same bait that was offered to Eve. Sure, there was pride in thinking we knew better than God but it went so much deeper than that. The motivation to act comes from a belief system held within. In other words, people sin to squelch the lie -- to bury it or disprove it. Without realizing it, they are acting on the lie and burying themselves instead.

Andrea

I thought about what we were saying, and I saw the same apple being fed to me. As a child, when my parents failed to address situations in the name of keeping the peace, they were feeding me the apple of, *you are not*

important enough to cause us such an embarrassing problem.
I spent my life eating that apple and believing daily that
I wasn't enough to count for an opinion or offer advice. I
didn't even believe I could trust my own feelings. I was not
enough to be regarded in any way. I wasn't enough when
I was single; I wasn't enough when I didn't have kids, or
if my house were a mess, the list never ended. There were
a million daily reminders of the apple I was fed. It was a
lie I accepted and ingested and suffered the consequences
of, though I had never fully understood my part in the
process. Repenting for my "sin" in general was done in
a blind submission to Christian traditions, with no real
knowledge of what actually brought me short of the glory
of God.

With each bite of the apple, I used self destructive
behaviors to find worth, happiness, or love. I began to
recognize those were the things I needed to find in myself.
Yet, I asked or demanded or hoped for others to do for
me what I could not and expected them to say the things
I did not feel so that I felt them. As the final layer was
removed exposing the deepest essence of my soul, I was
faced with a root of unworthiness which encapsulated my
needs and wants. Without value, I then had the desperate
need to create value or worth, searched for it, and thus was
destroying myself in the attempts.

Somewhere in my past, I learned a lesson of not being
worthy; I was fed the lie of not being enough. I listened to
the same subtle lie being whispered to everyone, man or
woman, since the beginning of time. This little inner voice
lead me to the decisions I thought would somehow make
me feel valued and loved or give me power because I really

felt powerless. Those choices were the gauze, ladder climbs, or façades; I understood *that* was the sin. If I valued myself when faced with any of those things, I, too, would have walked away.

It left me wondering, *If I still have the desperate need for worth, and everything I try leads to no-where, then what do I do to heal myself or feel whole?* It was the question we both knew, if answered, would change our lives. The answer was what my soul cried out for in the rain on Halloween night. It was what Andrea sought in the congregation or through performance for others. The answer was what we'd searched for in the bag of chips, in the mall, in the drug, behind the forced smile of a role, throughout the climb on the ladder. The answer was so profound it would reshape character, reframe the past, awaken the present, and renew the future. It became alive; we felt it bouncing off every cell in our bodies, tasting it, and letting it nourish. God.

Turning to God and seeing the lie for what it was, I realized what I needed all along. God was expecting me to stop trying to drown out the lie, stop numbing it away or attempting to disprove it. Expecting me to turn away from the emptiness of temporary living to find Him, He was waiting for me to see the lush bounty of life He had provided, a paradise within, and chose against the lie knowing I was enough. Fulfillment would have to and could only come through accepting God's abundant love of me. I had to trust that love enough to step out from behind the façade and be healed and measured as complete. Accepting the love opened my eyes to "the apple" that was always offered in its place. God's love completes and makes whole. I felt those words, those thoughts; they resonated like inscriptions on my heart. It was a moment of clarity, pure and full enough to change me. This knowledge swept over me like a wave rushing through, flooding me with profusion and towing away the debris. It was cleansing and renewing as I understood the message of God's love for the first time in my entire life.

Andrea

My tendencies dictated which I chose, but ultimately, like spokes emanating from the inner circle of a wheel, every act of sinfulness originated from the dark center of the same lie. It mattered little whether I operated along the spoke of gauzing, climbing, or being a face behind a wooden board; each was merely an outward act revealing the nature of the shadowy core of my life.

Identifying the lie dispelled the eerie darkness; accepting the love of God fanned the dying ember of my soul into flame, filling me with light. I saw God as encompassing enough to deliver me from the origin of the spokes, not the spokes themselves. That was why it didn't matter which outward expression of sin was chosen, though some choices carried harsher Earthly consequences than others; they were all manifestations of the same inner condition, my perceived lack of worth.

God never judged us harshly, but accurately, knowing the acts of sin were just different symptoms of the same inner darkness. *He desires for mankind to stop believing the lie, knowing it stands in the way of who we are created to be,* I realized.

I asked, "If the idea of not enough was indeed a lie, then did God come to pay for our not-good-enough-ness, or did He come to prove our worth?" We discovered the absolute relevance of the question. It was the only remedy to the poison permeating our systems from the apples we were fed.

Kimberly answered me perfectly conveying, "He came for both." I saw the sacrifice proving our value as well as ransoming our souls from death. I was aware of the point of Christianity, aware of what was missing, my soul and my worth, and freed from the fruitless cycle of searching for it.

He came to heal our wounds, the Artist's perfect statue was melted down to fill in the places in us left gaping from the ways we sought to remedy our feelings of inadequacy. I knew the burying of self was hiding what God had entrusted to me. Self was my soul, the part of me that would live forever. God had ransomed it from being eternally lost, buried, forfeited. He returned it to me to do with as He originally intended, without the fear and worry of judgment. It finally made perfect sense. For what good was it to gain the whole world, through attainment from gauzing or climbing, yet never feel whole? I would have lost my own soul, allowing it to remain hidden. Or what would I have given in exchange for my soul? No amount of affection, acceptance, or approval was worth trading myself for because I didn't find fulfillment in those things; none of it could help me feel my worth.

I'd lived my whole life around the concept of being ransomed with the life of the King and never realized I had value and worth far beyond what I could earn by sleeping with a boy to make him like me, being a perfect wife to make my husband happy, or even doing Christian work well enough to stand above the crowd. I didn't need to be popular or pretty, smart or funny. My worth was not found in my ability; I had value because I was created by God. I was chosen, loved, and purchased; God was pleased with me and glorified by me, simply because He made me. The choice to remain silent or to acquiesce was, in essence, falling short of who I was created to be.

Kimberly

It's knowing that my value comes from just being born, not rooted in the external, but in the eternal of who I am. Knowing that I am loved without question, and I am abundant through God's love. Without climbing over people, without shopping, without my image, without approval from others, and even without trying to squeeze that approval out of my father or Ed, I am whole. This freed and healed at the same time as I no longer needed to search for value, while recognizing the error in someone else seeking value through me. I was used as I had done the using in an effort to find the temporary fulfillment or wholeness without realizing my value was intrinsic from a never ending God.

The wages of sin is death suddenly meant something brand new. It was that the death was the death of self. The wages of sin would be death from whom I was created to be. I was not created to be aimlessly walking around the world grasping for love, acceptance, power, or whatever I could to find worth or purpose. When at the lowest point in my life the overwhelming feeling was not just loneliness or despair, but a feeling of death, of being bankrupt, that is the wage; the price paid for a buried life...the gig would be up. Learning to value myself as His creation meant I'd filled the void which had lingered my whole life, and I didn't have to pay that wage any longer. I would be alive in fullness, and sins would no longer be a dominating force in my life because I had value. I could rest. I could stop. I'd found peace.

Andrea

Stepping out of the prison I was in, I knew I'd never be the same. I was worthless apart from Jesus, not because I *was* worthless, but because I *believed* I was, and nothing could free me from the lie except perfect love. All the verses in the *Bible* about no one being worthy were there to point me away from looking to others for value. Those verses were there to direct me, not to further condemn me. If God did not value us, He would not have sent Jesus to buy us back when we were at our most sinful. The sacrifice *proved* our value. We had that worth when we were created; we just believed the lie blinding us to it.

I realized every one of us could find ourselves in the pictures of gauzing, ladder climbing, and the carnival cutouts, not to ruin us, but to make us aware of the flaw. We could stop breaking our promise to change because we could see why we acted that way and the real reason it made us fall short of God's glory. In acknowledging that we turned to the behaviors, we could see our need for forgiveness, but in knowing the *reason* we turned to the behaviors, we could see our need for value and love. We could be freed to live into what God had intended.

It was as if I had a Rubic's Cube twisted into color perfection and possessed the knowledge of how to put it back every time it became scrambled. The need to protect the one side I could figure out on my own was gone because I possessed the knowledge of how to fix my perspectives and realign what was happening to see the reason for my actions. I had been incapacitated to invest myself in anything that didn't bring me a feeling of value. It funneled me into groups and forced me into a lopsided lifestyle, because I could only compel myself to pursue the things which seemed capable of making me feel accepted, worthy, or valuable. Later, it would be apparent how I could have benefited from different choices, but at the time of choosing, I was blinded by my absolute addiction to what I thought would serve me in the moment.

The discovery was far more than an understanding of human behavior, of recognizing my own sin. It was an instant when I literally felt the repossession of my soul. Every part of me I had ignored, been ashamed of, forgotten, or lost, good and bad, was all returned to me to reacquaint myself with and to reassess. It was a feeling of and a knowing that I was filled, whole and forgiven. In that forgiveness, I was brought from feeling a lack of equity to knowing I had more value than I could express. It was with this awareness I would be who God was waiting to see. It was with this knowledge that I could discern between what would hide me, extinguishing my light, and what would make it shine like a city on a hill.

I was alive through an extraordinary significance, which could only come from deliberately accepting love. Love from other needy people or trusting in places and things could make us feel better for a while, but to experience freedom from want, to have the wound healed instead of gauzed up, the love had to be perfect. Perfect love takes away the fear of being judged. It frees us to be, say, and do without weighing ourselves in the arena of public opinion. Best of all it frees us from the endless frustration of being empty and in need.

Kimberly

The moment of realization that the love of God gave me value wherein by that love I would never need or want for worth again was life-changing. All the years and all the examples of erroneous effort led me trekking through life to find the answers. I saw my life as if from the top of a mountain; a huge mountain called "My Soul" to which I was at the peak. I could see the jagged rocks below me and barbed terrain of where I wandered. The spot I ran to in the storm on Halloween night left my imprints, my tears; they showed my nomadic path. Hallow, gapping voids, visible from where I gave away parts of myself, pitted the rough grade. I turned around on the summit to look at everyone I'd climbed over. They were bloody and stained with the sweat of my sins on them. Scraps of worn gauze were flapping in the breeze, as they had been torn off when they no longer stopped my pain. It looked like a patchwork of crusty fibers threaded throughout the uneven slope.

I looked at every part of my journey and fell to my knees finding the meaning of it all. It was as if everything in my life brought me to this moment. I was given value when I was created by God, created out of an abundance of love. He valued my existence, and knowing this cleansed the trampled Earth at my feet where I'd attempted to find that worth through the huge expectations on others, material possessions, and giving away parts of me until nothing was left. Standing at the crest, I could no longer be pulled down into that decaying landscape. I knew I could slip, even be pushed or fall, but I would rise up and reach the summit again because the strength of comprehending my worth from God was stronger than any force my life would encounter thereafter. I took a deep breath, a long gulp of freedom into my lungs. My eyes welled with tears, and I knew I was changed. Raising my head to the sky and letting the warmth flood into my body, I stood atop the mighty summit and felt the presence of God.

Chapter 12

Eve:
She Could Have Walked Away

Kimberly

The morning after our discovery, I busied myself in the kitchen as my kids dressed, ate and walked out of the door. They were still waving from the bus window as I dialed Andrea's number. She answered on the first ring, with an inquisitive, "Hello?"

"What just happened?" I asked disoriented. "My mind is wrestling with this concept, trying to comprehend what I think is the Message of God, the point of being a Christian." I had to stop talking. I sounded ridiculous.

Andrea jumped right in, "Can you be ready in 15 minutes? We need to talk this out."

Andrea

I had spent the night awake going over every *Bible* verse I had ever read or quoted or heard quoted to make further sense of what we discovered. The verses seemed to line up in my mind like a congregate of birds flying in harmonization across the sky. They all pointed, turned, dipped, and soared together to reach their destination. It was making more sense than I could have ever expected. It was peculiar and I felt a bit duped thinking over how often I must have missed the point.

Kimberly

We walked into the coffee shop just a few miles from Westbury. We hadn't said much on the ride over, the tension of waiting to talk becoming thicker as the minutes past. The cafe was quite a contrast from the restaurant we'd been in together the night before. It had wi fi capabilities and was thoughtfully designed with every flavor of coffee and biscotti to match the palates of the busy business people who came through the doors. I admired the confections behind the curved glass bakery case and chose a broccoli cheddar quiche and a raspberry torte. Andrea leaned in and ordered two buttery looking cookies with big chucks of grainy sugar on the top and two hazelnut coffees. She said it was her turn to buy.

We settled into a back corner booth and pressed into the tension. I started, "Did we just break through? Is the *apple concept* the complete answer?" I hoped she would tell me yes.

Andrea

I was glad to hear her give it a name: the apple concept. I smiled back dipping a cookie into my coffee, "Nothing has ever made more sense to me in my life." After taking a bite, I continued, "I think we need to talk to our pastor about it though, because it feels like a new way of looking at the Gospel."

Did it help to know there may be another level to the lesson; a less often discussed motivation for her act of prideful disobedience? We could only conclude, yes, but in doing so realized we were opening a Christian can of worms. The apple concept made sin relevant and could even explain how generosity could be evil, if the motivation were to fulfill a need for approval. It highlighted how judging others would be unreasonable given that what could be considered a sin for one may not be for another. The idea of personal value meant everyone had their own individual best and should be free to live into who God had created them to be: no pretence, no judgment, and no games.

Astonished by the multifaceted simplicity of the message, I admitted, "This inner realization of the truth sanctifies and makes free. It's not that we need a purpose or quest to find worth or love or any other God-like traits for our life. It's accepting they are already intrinsic." I knew it wasn't something often taught or mentioned as the slant is often toward thinking that finding Jesus will change us with some sort of spiritual hocus pocus. It leaves Christians thinking God didn't answer their prayers to be changed or that they should just try harder at *being* God-like. Again, I thought aloud, "Rather than 'getting' a godly character, it is a realization of being 'complete in Christ' already. There is a vast difference in those two approaches to true spirituality."

Kimberly nodded, "We had value all along."

Kimberly

Despite a life of paradise, Eve could still be temped into believing she was not enough, therefore leaving us with a *Biblical* account of the human condition. Whether taken as fiction or fact, the story provides a picture of God's abundant love and of man's inability to see that love, blinded by our desperate need for worth.

When together we dug down with psychology in one hand and God in the other, we connected the answer. The gauze, the ladder, and the carnival cut-outs, were lies used to remedy the belief of not good enough, the apples we were fed. Knowing that Jesus' death proved our worth, we could turn and walk away.

We needed not just psychology's self-esteem or God without understanding; we needed the synergy, the combining of the two. We needed the psychology and the spirituality; together they made the puzzle complete. Apart, the results would have never occurred, never connected for we only saw the world from our one dimension, one perspective. We needed each other to find the answers, but it required both of us to remain strong in our personal beliefs so that neither side would crumble. In doing so, the final outcome stayed preserved to become the river into which two tributaries flowed. The two smaller streams, which only served a piece of ourselves, were not strong enough to fully quench; but when combined into one mighty river, they became the water from which we would never thirst again.

Andrea

We got up to leave the café and noticed, Steve, the children's pastor from Old North Church. He was sitting with a few men just two booths away. He smiled at us,

"I waved over once, but you guys were really into a deep discussion over there. You've been here all morning!"

Kimberly answered back, "Well, when you're trying to save the world."

With a clever grin, I turned to whisper, "If he only knew."

We clearly had to gather ourselves. On the ride home Kimberly started singing a Christmas song. It was months past the holiday season, so I was sure there was more to her choice than I could figure at the moment. I listened as she piped,

"Long lay the world, in sin and error pining, till He appeared and the soul felt its worth..." Turning to look at me, she repeated in tune, "...and the soul felt its worth!"

I was astounded at the realization that we had listened to and sang those words, and the lyrics of many other songs, with little or no idea as to the fullness of their meaning. We couldn't help ourselves. We could have busted out the windows, "...A thrill of hope, the weary world rejoices. For yonder breaks a new and glorious morn..."

Kimberly

The day passed quickly as the apple concept continued transforming my thoughts. Our consideration slowly shifted to determining what we wanted to pass on to our children. I realized I wanted to do more than just tell them to avoid sinful behavior because it was the right Christian thing to do. While it may be well intentioned, it never seemed very successful. I called it "white knuckling" through life, because it's repeating in one's head, "I think I can, I think I can, I think I can." When I fail, I'll believe

God missed my prayers for strength, or I didn't pray hard enough; and I'll be full of guilt wondering, *Why I can't change.* The "white knuckle sermon" could work for a few people who could grip the wheel tightly enough to grunt out the lifestyle, but it wouldn't provide the full abundant life Jesus spoke about. Most of the people would feel bad that they couldn't live "a more Godly life" or adequately maintain their level of godliness. There was plenty of browbeating for everyone.

Had I understood my value was not wrapped up in others or in things, had I understood I was feeding myself a lie of not good enough on a daily basis, had I known Jesus came to save me from that lie and free me so I could be whole, I would have had a different life.

Andrea

Evenings were an anticipated time of solitude, and I was glad when my kids went to sleep without incident. After tucking the three of them into their beds, I crept down to the vacant living room. In the quiet seclusion, I stayed up meditating on the message of salvation. There was danger in attempting to sum it up in a short easy set of instructions, but I also knew how confusing it could be when people assumed the whole message was understood. It was the package I passed by as I boarded the Jesus train, the foundation I should have been building upon, but didn't realize I needed. I didn't know it even existed. Life without the rest of the message found me working and struggling to clean up my act without the understanding of why I made destructive choices to feel alive or gave myself up to others to feel purpose as I avoided living altogether. Bowing my head, I asked for a clear way to help my children comprehend how to accept His love.

Sitting in the dark, I realized God's Word had given us the best example. We were given a second chance to see ourselves as the man dying on the other side of Jesus. The thief, after taking responsibility for his situation, closed his eyes for the final time knowing his value was inside of himself. Demonstrating faith, he let go of the life he was losing. Asking Jesus to remember him, he said, "Please, remember *me*." He didn't say, "Please remember Yourself, or remember Your own goodness." He asked Jesus to see past the things he had done that brought him there to die that day, and Jesus did. Jesus saw the man inside, the one who never really understood what his own purpose was, the one who stole to satisfy a need or a want, but who found himself in emptiness facing the results of his choices. The thief woke up to the hope of Jesus accepting him as he was, broken and dying in shame, just maybe worth enough to be loved.

I knew it took faith to believe God's love was unconditional enough to trade His Son for me. It took faith to believe deep down I was worth saving and could feel whole from accepting that truth. It took faith to believe Jesus saw someone worth dying for inside of *every* human being, meaning we each have immeasurable value. This was the truth I needed to pass on to the kids; this was my faith. Walking upstairs, I felt a buoyancy I couldn't have created, an outlook I never could have imagined on my own.

Chapter 13

Naked:
Standing Alone In
Front of God

Andrea

In the morning, at the table in my kitchen, I took a deep breath letting all we'd discussed infuse my thoughts. I kept thinking about my brother, Richard, as if I somehow welcomed his opinions and the chance to thrash out the apple concept with someone else. I decided to write him a letter, but in my preparations of what to say, I realized we didn't know each other at all. Tapping the pen on the paper, I looked down at what I had written knowing it was more of the same broken ineffective stuff I'd always given to him in the past. I balled up the pink stationary and began again on regular notebook paper, reminding myself the letter was not about appearances. I wrote what would qualify as a journal entry and sent it.

Walking in with the mail days later, Tony admonished, "He's not going to write back, you know." It wasn't surprising when I didn't hear back from Richard; I had always loved him, but we were never more than strangers sharing a family. What found me unready was how it made me feel.

"Did I look like I was expecting mail?" I defended.

"I know you. You're expecting mail -- From Rich!" he said, sorting through the envelopes. Tony looked up from the pile and gave me the warm smile I'd come to appreciate as his way of letting me know he understood. "I just don't want you to feel bad."

At the sight of his kindness, I came unglued and broke down in tears, "I didn't send him a letter for a response, I mean, I did; but I thought he would want to have something…real." I wiped my face and walked into the powder room for a tissue. Walking in behind me, Tony wrapped his arms around my waist hugging me while I blew my nose. I wanted to yell at him to give me privacy, but I knew I was just frustrated about my brother. "I feel ridiculous," I cried.

Thinking about my brother took a lot more out of me than I wanted to acknowledge. I needed to figure out how in the world I was going to live without knowing him as well as I wanted to. The following afternoon, in the study off my bedroom, I dropped into the chair and opened my journal; I wrote:

I imagine my soul floating around without a body. If I were alone, without Tony and my kids, if I couldn't say the word "neighbor" or talk about

Kimberly at all -- and my brother was equally stripped of recognizable outer features, would we be able to identify each other in a crowd of other souls? I don't think we would.

To find myself I had to lose the identity I hid behind. To find others, I feared I would have to wait. In the after light of my new way of living there was a shadow of pain since I could not uncover others as I had myself. When I heard the mail truck, I shut the journal and promised myself, *Today will be the last time I check for an answer.*

Kimberly

Hearing Andrea's iron mailbox close with a clank, I stepped out of the garage shielding my eyes from the sun. It was one of those classic warm afternoons toward the end of winter just as spring was breaking. People wanted to be outside tasting the fresh air, breathing new life again. Neighbors were working in their yards, and I had been sweeping out my garage.

Andrea yelled across resigned, "I'm done waiting. I'll have to try something different."

I walked over and stood along the mushy tree lined curb. I wanted to offer her my condolences or apologies, but it was out of my hands. It had nothing to do with me, although I could relate to people in my own life from whom I felt just as separated.

Andrea

As we walked toward the house, Kimberly quietly allowed me to turn the discussion away from the letter I didn't receive. I told her, "I've been thinking about people in such a different way since waking up to all of this. It's both comical and sad." Stepping up to the front porch, I described how leaders like my aunt stand gallantly at the head of a group, where they are hailed and revered, and I said, "Think of people as lights. I mean, imagine each of Nora's followers holding up a dim mini-Christmas bulb trying to cast enough glow to make her feel important. In turn, she holds an old welcome light over their heads." My mind pictured her highlighting certain hardworking members making them feel special. I could see them straining to stand under her approval; straining to be cast upon with light so they would also feel important. I added, "There's a king in the Bible who commanded the subjects to bow to a statue he commissioned of himself, as if all those people directing attention on his image could strengthen his soul, or bring him glory." I thought how I wanted Tony to hold his light to me and make me feel bright, or how I was one of the followers who craved the welcome light to shine above my head as I served in the cult-church.

Kim interjected, adding, "When we don't comprehend our worth, we do what we can to gain the faint flicker of temporary human approval. We have to convince ourselves we have worth, and for some it takes gaining a following."

"Exactly!" I agreed, "But our lights are for something infinitely more important." Sitting on one of the glider chairs on my porch, tilting my face toward the warmth, I continued, "What if there is a flame inside of each of us that is like our fingerprint and is recognizable to God? Imagine what it feels like in heaven when a light is obscured. Imagine when it is aiming away from Him toward another human being or object." I traced my finger through the winter's dirt on the little table on the porch, guessing, "What if a hush falls in Heaven as He waits. Like in the movies, people are in the control room silent and scared. They know they have lost contact with a member of their group, and they fear the worst." I described the way they wait and hope while the minutes pass like hours. Then, miraculously, there is a blip on the radar, a trace of who they are hoping to find. They erupt into cheers, clapping and hugging as they watch the light glowing on the screen moving closer to them.

Kimberly put her hand to her forehead like she was checking for a fever, "We have to ask ourselves, can God see *my* light or is He scanning the Earth trying to find a trace of me?" Brushing back her hair and growing more agitated with the wind, she said, "Am I hidden under actions and reactions based upon other people's opinions or looking to stand under the artificial glow of a career, a custom home, wanting it to be my light? Is the person I would be, if I were stripped of opinions or roles, visible to the world?" Her questions were sounding more like irritated statements, until she had a realization, "*That* is the person who will stand in front of God one day, alone. Should I just show up, a bunch of apples in my extended arms, and drop them at His feet?"

Kimberly sat at the edge of her chair turning toward me like an attorney giving her final closing remarks, "Who is the gauzing alcoholic with no bottle in his hand, the ladder climber with no boasting rights, the carnival cut-out without the image they created for themselves?"

"Yes!" I exclaimed, "Who are the wealthy when alone in front of God with no money? I never thought of standing on my own, standing up all alone in front of God, having no church to boast of, no family to point to, no house, money, friends...

"I will be naked, alone in front of God," I said, realizing the impact of that statement. "Who will I be? Will He recognize me from seeing my light shining every time He looked for it? Will He see that I cared about other people enough to interrupt the gauzing to know them?" I stood taking a step toward the edge of the porch. Balancing with my toes over the side, the drop to the ground made me dizzy. I whispered, "Or will He say, 'I was hungry, lonely, thirsty... but you couldn't stop numbing and posturing and hiding long enough to notice'." As I spoke, the words felt so real, an accusation I wouldn't be able to hide from, or justify if left unsettled.

Kimberly

Watching Andrea steady herself on the edge of her porch, I asked, "What if we knew how much time we had left of our lives?" She looked over her shoulder at me almost losing her footing. I watched, thinking of the delicate balance between life and death admitting silently, *In the end, will the things we want to be remembered for be exemplified in what we give our attention to now?* I wondered aloud, "As I lay dying, will I call for my car, my business, try to keep up an image, remember some abuse I held on to? Will I look to gently squeeze the hands of the people who knew me and loved me and were part of shaping my life, and I theirs? Would my love for them show through my life experiences?"

I thought a lot about the people around me, some family, some friends, and some just strangers, who all displayed, in varying degrees, a seeking for worth. Thinking of different relatives, one gauzing away his pain through a bottle of whiskey, one eating her emotions until she weighed 300 pounds, I wondered, *Would they ever accept that they were substituting temporary things for the love of an infinite God?* If I could tell my neighbor she didn't have to try to keep up with everyone she met because she was already a valued woman, maybe she wouldn't exhaust herself trying to keep up status. If I could explain to the stranger in church who over-volunteered with a forced smile, that she was worthy of saying no, maybe she would have the confidence to know her worth was not wrapped up in her church-image. There was story after story, person after person, looking for what I knew to be true, not knowing they were enough.

Unable to fall asleep, I laid in the dark remembering the words out of Jesus own mouth. He said He'd come to give life so that we could live abundantly. I wanted that for everyone, no matter what their circumstances, I wanted people to feel complete within. Wishing I could just give this new bountiful life away to whomever was just as lost as I once was, I asked God to give me patience and guidance knowing I had no idea how I was going to live out this love.

Choreographing a dance in my mind was my standard sleep inducer. This night, it was more lyrics than movement that came to life. Like a dance, I paced out words to express my feelings as they formed into a verse.

In my dream, I could see your dark, deep set eyes and I had to approach.

You did not look up, but you could sense my presence as I bent down to be near.

I touched your face and peered into those pulling eyes.

Their words cried out as lost, abandoned, overflowing fear.

"Do you not know you shine?" I whispered through the stinging wells that drew.

"Do you believe that you and I are one, not two?"

If you could only view within my grasp I hold
The light, the beauty, of a soul foretold.

In my dream, you recoil unable to accept my bequest
But I cannot give what lies beneath the pain of these
Feeble beliefs and diminished lights of a spirit
Wherein the truest love is found and frees.

I see the starvation and pour in the nourishment of love
Knowing that mine alone is inadequate and must come from above.

But in the decant, the drought has not allowed for

abundant take

So once again you seem to accept your fate.

In my dream, I asked the shriveled pile of being
"can you remember when you knew you were whole?"
Shifting in the stacks and swells, I watched her try to
gather, pulling in around her what was left of her life...her
soul.

With head bowed, I heard a "no" in a gentle tone
Ruffling, awkward; her seemingly alone.

Never catching my gaze, not another word
It was the only sound from the being I heard.

In my dream, I dropped in the can what I could
Aching, still, for more to share
Aching, still, wanting more to give...
Aching, still, wanting her to love and care.

"Find your light, my friend," I uttered taking steps away.
"I hope to meet you, fully, in another day."
The dark eyes followed my reproach then fell
Asleep in the lost world in which she dwells.

The reality was we were living in a broken world, but I was no longer broken. I was certain a day would come where I would stand alone in front of God, naked in that I would be stripped of the images, roles, and past hurts that defined me. The lies gone, I knew I would want to have lived with the understanding of my worth from God. I would want to know I was given life and became alive in the fullness He created for me. If my life, all life, began with a lie believed because of not being enough, a need to be better, then I was determined to go back to the genesis of that lie for myself and acknowledge my value. As I drifted off to sleep, I promised myself, *I won't allow others to obscure my light or smother it or abuse it, and I won't allow myself to ignore it. In God, with God, because of God...I am enough.*

Section 3

Nourished by Truth

Chapter 14

Victims:
The Bitter Taste of Blame

Andrea

I stopped in at my mom's new condo for dinner. She had moved just miles away, and it was nice having her close enough that I could visit often. Sitting on the breezy porch surrounded by delicious food felt like a Mediterranean vacation. Tilting back in our chairs, we gave in to the opportunity of simple small talk. Nonchalantly, my mom unfolded a story from her childhood I'd never heard, but it provided one of the last links needed to connect the scenarios of my life. Her story was a gift. She began, "I was so smart in school. I always made straight A's; I could spell any word."

"You got straight A's?" I asked.

"Yeah, but I gave up hope and quit trying when I

realized it really didn't matter," she admitted in defeat.

"What made you think it didn't matter?" I demanded.

She answered with a shake of her head, "Your Aunt Nora was so brilliant in home economics." She leveled her gaze, "Now you have to realize the times we lived in, but she was so gifted. She won a contest, which gave away a full scholarship to a local college to study home economics. It was really an accomplishment. I was so proud of her."

She went on to explain how the only expense her sister was required to pay was a registration fee of $150.00. When the representatives from the scholarship committee came to their home to present the award and have the papers filled out, my grandfather refused to pay the fee. He pounded the old wooden table in their kitchen and told them to leave. Throwing his hands in the air in disgust, he wanted to know why anyone thought he should pay $150.00 to send his daughter to learn how to cook and keep house if she already knew enough to win their silly contest.

He fed her the apple. When he told her school was not worth $150.00, he was essentially saying, "You aren't worth $150.00." My aunt had no way of paying the fees in time and so lost out on her chance to go to college. My mom concluded then, when she was just in high school, that it made no sense to try to be the best student she could because even if she had the chance of a lifetime, it would slip away from her, too.

After visiting late into the night, my mom walked me to my car. The midnight streets were abandoned, and on the lonely ride home, I thought about how Nora had to let go of her dream to go to college, and then demonized college for everyone else. My heart sank as I wondered,

Did she have to cross off school, dismissing it as evil and out of God's will, to lessen the pain of losing the chance to go? Rolling to a stop at an empty intersection, under a blinking yellow caution light, I knew she had fallen victim to the apple she was fed, only to then feed it to me. I caught my breath and suddenly realized I didn't need to stop. I pressed through hearing broken glass crackling under the weight of my car.

Faulting my Aunt Nora for how I performed as a Christian cut-out or for discouraging me from earning an education made it easy to pass off my responsibility for giving myself away. In my mind, she'd become the enemy who kept me from happiness. I noticed how the ultimate destination of every choice I'd made was to blame another person or God for how it did or didn't turn out. Without accepting those results were because of my own behaviors, I became a victim.

Kimberly

Awaking to the understanding of what love could do for us freed us from the sin cycle, but we were left with the fruits of past decisions and what to do about them. The weight and poor health of overeating, the stress of financial problems from overspending, broken relationships from ladder climbing, and all the other burdens that accompany desperate choices, this was how I woke up. There were also things beyond our control, those abuses done to us that we had no way of choosing against. We had to accept there was no magic wand, no Jesus genie coming to make it all go away. If our hope rested in a reset button, we would have been disappointed for sure.

As the sun rose flooding my family room with light, I sank into the corner chaise lounge. Thinking of every way I'd sought validation by gauzing and ladder climbing, I couldn't recall if it was conscious or not, but I became more and more disillusioned hoping *this year, this house, or this job* would be the one to bring me the true happiness or the validation I craved. I could see how, once all the sin outlets became exhausting enough, resentment set in. I had known many people twice my age, who were so angry and bitter, thinking the world just did them wrong. They were frustrated from never getting the results they hoped for.

Our default responses were based upon what we believed would constitute a good life. There were as many notions of the ideal life as there were people in the world because every human being grew up eating the apple of …*This will make you better.* The *"this"* could vary in any given household. With the perfect life in mind, the images we sought to aspire to, hide behind or distract ourselves from were setting us up for disappointment. No life plays out exactly as planned, so as our fantasies failed to become reality, we lived in a state of disillusionment.

It was like I had orchestrated my own life away from God and toward an assembly of people and things I needed to keep my spirit in harmony. I wanted the flute people to sing out happiness, the drum people to excite me, the slide trombone players to make me laugh, and the saxophone players to romance me. I wanted to direct each section by stepping onto my podium and pointing my need wand to whatever section fulfilled me at the moment. I expected the people to work in concert to play out the score, and if someone didn't perform to my expectations, they messed with my desperation for accord. As the conductor of my own life, I felt owed this picture of happiness, and wondered why others failed to do their part to bring it to fruition. The world became a violent concert where every note assaulted my senses when even strangers seemed to be against me.

I realized, the more we struggle to create our ideal, the more we destroy the people in our lives with the weight of our expectations on them, which ultimately devastates those relationships. Never understanding God was the conductor and my needs were already met, I became upset at the orchestra for their poor performance. All I had to do was listen to the beauty of the world God created for me, listen to the concertos of others, which are for their purposes and to God's glory not mine. I needed to learn to play out my own life in harmony, and stop trying to force others into making me feel less empty. Of course, at the time of my conductorship, I thought I was right. "Places everyone...places."

Andrea

As Kimberly and I reasoned together about trying to conduct our lives, I wanted to believe I had been made to perform in the selfish symphonies of others around me. Visible gestures, narrowed eye contact, and audible sniffs had once sent me into furious performance. I never saw myself as a conductor, but it was like holding a mirror to a mirror and looking into infinity. The awful score I'd composed and sought to conduct was to be the second chair in someone else's Opus.

It was clear that if we could all blame each other or the world, we wouldn't have to face our choices or examine our attitudes. We could continue to sleep through the reasons and the answers with them, stripping ourselves of the opportunity for personal insight. Worse still, we would go on trying to live into the life we'd imagined for ourselves instead of the life we were actually given. If I had not turned inward to dig out the truth, I would have kept waiting for the people in my life to fix themselves to make me happy. I would have continued trying to please others in the ways they expected and so the lie would have continued to bury me, as my soul song went unheard.

Kimberly

I once thought I'd never experienced envy, but I was not aware of the entire definition. Envy is the resentful, unhappy feeling of wanting somebody else's success, good fortune, qualities, or possessions. It is the observable end result of not making the most of the life we've been given, the life entrusted to us. If we failed to become who we were supposed to be, or if we measured ourselves by the world around us, we were destined to become bitter toward the good and goods of others. Part of the significance of envy is thinking, *Why do they get to have something I can't.* It's the "life's not fair" mantra taken personally, and instead of accepting our own blessings and pitfalls, and how we can be responsible in part for both, we allow the difficulties to make us victims. If we wallow long enough, seeking fulfillment from things incapable of providing, we not only end up exhausted but also frustrated and angry at the notion of others happiness or success or misperceived lack of problems. We think God is answering other people's prayers, while we keep moving to the end of the line. Envy becomes a voice of justification saying, "If I can't have this…I'll take that!"

Evidence of this was everywhere: the one night stand, the passed-out drunken night out, buying the $200.00 pair of shoes we can't afford, or inflicting a verbal vomit rage on our loved ones. We don't realize the victimization is, to a large degree, self induced. We believed the lie and then, began sinning to "fix it," wallowed in unfulfillment when our efforts failed, became resentful, bitter, and envious toward the people in our lives, who we were expecting to make it all better.

It was the explanation of the life of *my* generous aunt, who lived 68 years, the last 30 as a bitter, angry woman. She tried for 15 of those years to have children but never could; then, her husband died tragically leaving her a childless widow. My aunt was an outward, bubbly woman who loved to eat ice cream and drink tea out of fancy cups. She had an "outfit" to wear everyday with matching purse, shoes, and lipstick. She was social and involved with charity work and had lots of lady friends, as she liked to call them. However, she held on to the pains and hurts of life in a file system, opening them often, even daily. Anger built up in her heart until it eventually became bitterness.

She kept track of how many days went by without someone calling her or visiting. Gossiping about other family members and playing the victim role overtook her personality, until they were all that was left. Nobody ever met her huge expectations or showed her the appreciation she craved and wanted. The slow waitress, the restaurant that served lukewarm potatoes, the boy who cut her grass too low, nobody provided her the quality results she demanded. The world "owed" her and never measured up. The stress of envy clogs life, and without ever knowing her worth, she died at the young age of 68 from a stroke. The realization that Jesus did not die on the cross so that she would have an emotionally barren life escaped her to the end. He wanted her to live fully, to see both herself and others through His loving eyes. Unfortunately, even as a faithful, church-going Christian, she lived without understanding the message of God.

Andrea

We were learning from people in ways I was sure they never intended. Considering our aunts, it seemed Kimberly's aunt had become a victim, hardened by bitterness, and my aunt had given over to the side of envy that purposed in its heart, *If I can't have it, no one should!* I had to face how she had used me to build an alternative dream to soothe the wound from the apple she'd ingested from her father. My eyes were opened to the way she accepted the lie of not being worthy of college and allowed it to become the rotten green apple of envy. I had eaten that same apple when it was repackaged as a decree that school was a waste of time for women. Crying out to God, I sought the strength to break the cycle and bear real fruit, the kind the *Bible* promises we can.

I finally understood the purpose of confessing my sin to God. Repentance was taking responsibility for my part in any given situation. It wasn't that God was holding things against us until we listed them out in humiliation. It was that we were caught in never ending patterns until we recognized them, became accountable for our choices, and trusted God enough to walk away from those behaviors. I could never truly be free from a tendency until I recognized my blame and admitted to my part in the process. If seeing myself as a victim was a dead end path that brought me to bitterness and envy, the only way out was to turn and go the other way. I had to stop fueling the cycles I hoped would somehow end because the result of never taking onus for my own life was to blame others, a condition for which there is no remedy.

Kimberly

Welcoming insight and being thankful for the opportunity to know better and to do better was the *only* remedy, which meant the opposite of envy was grateful. Gratitude was the antidote for a life infected with a root of bitterness. Once I understood God's loving intention for my life and allowed Him to restore me, my perceptions changed. I awoke to the blessings surrounding me; my family always loved me, I had great kids, and a nice American life. However, I'd gained a keen awareness of the danger in thinking, *Why me or why can't I*. I saw the danger of self-indulgent sin, and how my critiques on others were another way of trying to level them into my pit of discontent.

My focus had come away from being the victim and toward being my best self, being grateful for the blessings of others even when it was what lacked in my own life, and continuing to pray for wisdom and guidance in re-directing my life away from self pity to strength in God.

Being a victim is a position of weakness. It was admitting to oneself *I am powerless*. Reclaiming my life, I could humbly admit the apple I was fed, and the apple I fed to myself, was out of unawareness of God's abundant love. His strength gives me strength to turn back to my family, children and spouse and attempt a better life, attempt to be treated differently and give of myself differently. Knowing what He'd taught us, Andrea and I had to rebuild a stronger root base in which to live out the apple concept. We hoped our families would be there to help support us as we struggled to grow, as we struggled to resist the apples that would dangle in temptation before us still whispering the lie...*and this will make you better.*

Andrea

In discussing gratitude, it became clear that considering the blessing propelled us toward our desired goals. It didn't mean I had to thank God for tragedy or illness, but accept my life as it was, taking responsibility for the things I caused knowing those were the things I could change, and admitting there were certain misfortunes beyond my control. I was not a victim. I didn't need to take a national average for what issues I was facing and decide if they were fair or not. My best option was to find the opportunities within my own life. Recognizing the benefit of and seizing the information, help, and comfort available allowed me to operate with forward motion rather than rotting in dissatisfaction. Essentially, walking away from the mindset of powerlessness was a choice.

Clearly, God had not created us with a flaw, but we grew up adopting the lie as an unfortunate inevitability. We abdicated our worth based upon interactions with our parents, then friends, or teachers, and ultimately our spouses. Though they each may have played a part in exposing us to the apple or benefiting from our ingestion of it, we had a choice in allowing it to define us. Our reactions to these broken relationships carried us through life strengthening our belief that we should have been or could have been someone or something other than who we were created to be. We listened to the whispers influencing us to beg for and demand attention and approval, the undertone which fooled us into burying ourselves beneath performance or expectation. The painful truth was we handed over our value because we wanted to feel something that was within us all along. I came to believe, at the core of who we are, there is a hunger for spiritual understanding, but when we feel the pangs, if we acknowledge them, it is the moment of spiritual conception.

Kimberly

I remember being pregnant and feeling my child grow from within, kicking, flipping, and sleeping in the cocoon-like atmosphere. The first breath of life comes with pain and screaming and an emergence into the intense and fearful light. New life begins. Despite my emotional meltdowns, with God, I found myself immersed in light. Because I knew nothing of what was changing in me, I became afraid and weighed down, feeling my natural tendencies wanting to take me back to the warmth of the familiar. I had to struggle at times to breathe from the overwhelming weight of the adjustment. I had to learn how to live all over again, how to respond, and how to speak. Knowing all I had to do was take small steps, one at a time, in the right direction, helped lessen the doubt of whether or not I could live a different life. It's living with soul value: A life which has nothing to do with excess, power, fear, or greed, not programmed or legalistic, and not lived through victimization. Each day was a process I had to stay committed to and understand above all else, I could do it. I realized, with strength in God all things were possible.

Andrea

Empowerment meant moving toward that life of soul value. To do so, I had to place God's intended *me* in the center of my mind. I had to choose what would develop those personal, intricate qualities of individualism that glorified Him as my Creator -- and what would stunt them and cause me to fall short. The idea of our relationships with God being personal was evident in the fact that what caused me to be *me* may not be what was best for someone else. Figuring out who I was, what God looked for in *me*, was a challenge.

Kimberly

Seeking ways of putting our experiences into words, I came to the definition of betrayal and was shocked to read: to be disloyal or false around. The words jumped off the page. To be false around was a betrayal. The description converged on me like a stale pocket of dead air from my old way of thinking. People deserved to have authentic relationships with each other, as painful or embarrassing or as fearful as it would feel, they were entitled to genuineness. Otherwise, those relationships would be betrayals. I would even be betraying myself.

I recalled the eerie dream of the buried girl in the bloody white dress, and how I had murdered her. I thought of the way I had lived in fear behind a façade, always wondering when I would be exposed for committing a crime I didn't even understand. Knowing what I had done to myself and why, exhumed the innocence and brought a once unrecognizable face out into the warmth of the sun. Healed from the brutality of incompleteness and free from fear, I was alive and determined to walk on in the light. Baring the scars, the wounds would no longer carry their once fatal consequences. Aware of the results of betrayal I would move forward with the strength to choose against a life of duplicity.

After grasping the apple concept and accepting my value from God, some of my relationships would have to change. Some would end. Some could blossom. I knew instantly I was yet again different, somehow stronger than I was just moments before. It reminded me of becoming a mother. I was the same person at 10:14pm when the doctor placed my first born into my arms as I had been at 10:13pm, but forevermore, I would be considered a mom.

In that same way, the understanding of who I was left me no other options than to materialize that self into my everyday life. I could no longer fret over if I was enough, what I wished I was, or what I never became. Given this definition, it was a betrayal to my family every time I was not strong enough to bear my thoughts, opinions, wants, or flaws, every time I held in how much I loved them out of awkwardness and every time I was deeply hurt and didn't stand up for myself. Sharing the truth of who I was, discussing my desires, my regrets, and my hopes was part of the life of freedom I'd gained. Pretending was an insult to who they were; they deserved the dignity of honesty. I deserved the dignity of being honest with myself.

Andrea

Once again I thought of a *Bible* verse and wondered if this idea of betraying ourselves and our loved ones was what the Psalmist meant when he wrote that God wanted us to have truth in our inward parts. *Was he telling us to be honest with ourselves, and so with the people we claimed to love?* How uncomplicated and beautiful and real it was to be unselfish in a confident display of humility. I never would have believed the path to glorifying God would be found through living as myself in testimony to the One who designed me. We had rewritten our dream, unearthing ourselves from the suffocation of spiritual death to come alive in the knowledge of God's love and truth.

In this new life, faith without works made absolute sense. It was astonishing to realize it did no good for me to say I believed God had adopted me as His child, if I still traded myself for the esteem of others or even tried to impress God with my efforts. I was released from the burden of duty and performing good deeds and freed to act and react naturally without excessively calculating what He would expect. The works would be actions in keeping with my completeness, and they were not always going to be Christian acts of service. My faith worked into my life when I was brave enough to live out my wholeness in every way I could.

Being a people-pleaser seemed very Christ-like, so changing felt like a huge sin, especially when it meant arguing with my husband, sister, children… or confronting a neighbor or relative for things I normally would have sent underground, thinking I'd forgiven. I felt spoiled and ungrateful when I asserted myself about things I would usually have deemed "not worth fighting over." I awoke further to just how much of a rut we were attempting to bump out of. Every one of us was guilty of contributing to the habit of our relationships. Deciding how much I could demand or expect or desire from my family was incredibly intimidating, and I knew I'd reverted to the fog a few times already. My tendencies to sin were being coaxed along by my unknowing loved ones, as they fought to keep things the same. It was also the first time I understood the women of the seventies having to leave home to "find themselves." The effort it would take to break through the expected behaviors made me think about life alone. I wondered if it would be easier to be free and real if I were by myself, and I was glad to remember the *Bible* says that once we love God, focused on Him, the most important thing we can do is love the people we share our lives with.

For me, being who I was created to be would be done

from the life I'd made. Facing Tony in the living room before bed, I thought of my relationships as a sort of old building undergoing renovation. Each relationship was a room badly in need of repair. Some of the work could be done simultaneously and with ease, a tearing down of walls. The clean up was going to be more of an effort, as I would ask for and make apologies as needed. Building is specific to each separate space, and I'd have to pay attention to the details. There was joy in knowing I didn't have to stay in a dilapidated mess waiting for someone else to decide what to do about it.

Tony was keeping pace with the changes asking me questions and learning what I thought. I was finding out more about him than I realized there was to know. However, fighting for my marriage to be a great example of what God intended sometimes would mean fighting with Tony. It wouldn't be poetic or romantic at those times, but it was going to be beautiful because it would be real. What we chose to build was no longer the *picture* of the perfect marriage, it was the marriage itself.

Chapter 15

Forgiveness:
Jesus Was a Rock Star

Kimberly

Running through the house putting away shoes and calling for the kids to pick up their bookbags, I peeked into the pot on my stove and laughed at the chicken simmering in the soup. I was cooking more than I ever had, deciding all I needed was a good recipe. I phoned Andrea to see if she and the kids wanted to eat with us because Tony and Ed were going to another long township meeting. We used any excuse to hang out and talk.

Coming through the front door, Andrea's kids dropped their jackets to the floor and kicked their shoes off into a pile on top of them. Tripping over the mess, they bolted up the stairs to play.

Andrea wondered, "Why do kids disregard everything

they've been taught?" Exasperated, she scooted the mound out of the way so she could close the door.

"Please," I sighed, "I just did the same thing minutes before you got here...It's endless." Walking into the kitchen I glanced over at the timer on my oven counting down two minutes left on the brownies I was baking for dessert. "I made soup, and I didn't waste any of the meat," I said in jest remembering the day she came over to teach me and I couldn't stomach eating the carcass once cooked.

"It smells delicious," she complimented as I grabbed a ladle and stirred the pot one last time.

Andrea

Kimberly was a fantastic cook; her chicken noodle was some of the best I'd ever had. As we sat at the glass top table in her kitchen sipping the steaming broth, I was ready to talk about forgiveness. It was the natural progression after the discovery, like the splitting open of a buried seed. A shoot of life emerged outward, leaving the effects of the cold and the dark so the newness could not only be felt but seen.

There were two sides to forgiveness, and the problem for me had always been living with only half of the forgiveness message. My sister and I joked someone could park on one of our feet, and we would just smile politely and wait, hoping they wouldn't take too long to roll away. I knew God wanted me to be longsuffering, but I didn't know how long, how forgiving. I thought as long as I tried to ignore the offenses and pretend I wasn't hurt, irritated, or angry I was being like Jesus. I had to stop feeling in order to convince myself I was forgiving, so my wrong idea of forgiveness left the offenders without remedy, and kept me dormant.

I explained to Kimberly how seeing myself as the restored bronze statue showed me I did not have to quietly take it while another person sinned on me; that was not how Jesus acted. In the Gospels, He *was* who He *was*. When He wanted to expound on scripture in the temple, He didn't feel inadequate because He was only twelve-years-old. When He wanted to spend time with tax collectors and prostitutes, He didn't care who thought He was a "winebibber." If He needed a break from the crowd, He took it. When He was sad, He wept. Jesus never let the Pharisees intimidate Him into cowering under them. When He was angry, He turned over the tables in the temple. When throngs of people surrounded Him like He was a rock star, He didn't let His close friends tell Him He was too important to go to Jerusalem to die. He forgave them, but He didn't do what they wanted, until it was in line with His purpose.

Being like Jesus was not always about silently dying in front of people. In fact, I was seeing how His was the only sacrifice that could save others. When I martyred myself for the sake of those around me, it took Jesus out of the equation. I had sacrifices and choices to make, but they should never have robbed people of the opportunity to grow and change because I was too afraid of looking unforgiving. That was keeping people back and placing myself in God's role. Allowing others to sin on me stood against everything Jesus did.

Kimberly

The other half of the forgiveness message I was ready to hear was a from the heart effort to let go. I told Andrea, "We have to protect our own lights and those of our children if we have them, but once we've moved away from letting someone sin on us, we have to let go." She nodded her consent, as I insisted, "One must view the individual, whether ourselves or another, as loved and accepted by God just as they are currently, even if that person is buried under a pile of sinful actions."

I knew the only bona fide way to "let go" was love, a love not defined as a feeling, an action, or a decision, but a perception. The perception of human beings as God sees us, forgiving us because we "know not what we do." It takes strength to convey the loving message, "I will not tolerate certain behaviors in my life any longer." But stepping back and away, that same strength can instill in them a reason to change. Such action submits to God's control, releasing me from the prison of martyrdom and the burden of being the victim of another's sin.

Andrea

Agreeing with Kimberly I said, "You know, the *Bible* does say when we refuse to forgive another person we, ourselves actually become imprisoned." It reframed my experience of serving at my aunt's church. "Forgiveness is recognizing the human propensity to hurt, use, and abuse, but hoping for truth to set the offender free."

"Yes," Kimberly added, "forgiveness sees the soul bound behind the sin and loves that soul, wanting to see it shine in glory to God."

By forgiving, I was not setting myself above the other person, saying, "I pardon you," in a pious, self-righteous way. Instead, I should acknowledge our equality. I knew sitting there in Kimberly's kitchen, the significance of Christ taking on flesh and living among us. He brought us to where He was, by lowering himself. He offered us the opportunity to humble ourselves, accept His love, and be freed. His death also served as an outward sign of what sin does to the human soul, murders it, leaves it buried. It was something we should not want for anyone.

Walking home, I stopped in the street turning to look back at Kimberly's big, brick home. The golden glow of lights from within fell onto the yard outside. Knowing the light inside of me was finally glowing brightly enough to illuminate some of the world around me, I decided on the occasions when I would see my aunt, like weddings or extended family reunions, I would treat her with kindness. I would love her, forgiving her for feeding me the apple. I would hope for her to unearth the lie in her life, to find freedom, and to finally see herself as valuable to God without feeling she had to perform well to earn His approval.

I went straight up to my sitting room, still wearing my jacket. Digging through boxes of old photographs, I found a picture of her as a very young child. I rubbed my thumb across the glass of the tiny frame, looking at the photo of a beautiful innocent girl with thick, black hair and dark Italian skin. Down in the kitchen, I rearranged things to make a place for it on the window sill. Thanking God, I prayed that seeing her everyday as someone's daughter would remind me how she too was fed an apple, a lie which shaped her life. I stood back from the window trying to relate to the little picture thinking, *The two things connecting everyone in the world are the wound that's killing us and the Love Who seeks to heal us.*

Kimberly

In looking at my every hurt or every wound, I could see none of it was personal. Although it was done to me, it was not because of me. This was so monumental to my healing and desire to forgive. I saw how the hurts I endured were someone else's attempt to use me as gauze or climb over me. I wanted to rent a billboard or shout to the world, "We are all universal in our need for value." Knowing that allowed me to understand how the need, the bleeding out need for value in each of us dominates clear rational thought. As long as we live excessively, preoccupying ourselves with obtaining more material worth, or verbally abuse and gossip our inadequacies away by keeping people down, we can distract ourselves from the need. We can force up another rung or smile once again through the cut-out, without realizing the impact of our choices on the people who share our lives. These actions leave our spouses, our kids, our parents, and our friends caught in the crossfire of our worthlessness. Never feeling enough, we inadvertently take it out on everyone. The need came first.

Since I knew none of my neighbors were out to hear my late night sermon, I turned my realization back inward. I needed to look to seek forgiveness because my shout out came with an echo reverberating and forcing me to listen to my own words. I admitted to hurting and using others in my own futile attempts at fulfillment. My father loved me and worked hard his whole life to provide me with a fun childhood filled with vacations and traditions. My mother gave me everything she had even going to college to become a nurse when I was in junior high, so they could afford dance lessons. Ed was a good husband and generous father, building family rooms, and keeping our home in top shape. I expected them to complete in me something they couldn't, and I thought their flaws prevented my happiness. It angered me, made me resentful; I saw myself as a victim of their behavior. Having no foundation to draw upon to rescue me from the anxiety, fear, depression, and worthless feelings, I expected my family to save me from them. *Maybe the one I need to forgive the most is me,* I considered.

Knowing how we are all equal helps to forgive. Looking at my distorted reflection in my bedroom window, I thought about deeper wounds and how they could seem impossible to let go. I'd seen the horrors that could be done to others; everyone has. For me though, letting go didn't condone or accept those horrors but allowed me to move on from them. *One day,* I told myself, *I will meet God and need the forgiveness granted way more than I must deliver it out in my life.* I knew I couldn't ask for it if I didn't give it. I knew when I stood alone in front of God; I wouldn't be naked, as much as I would be covered in forgiveness.

The headlamps of Ed's car distracted me as they momentarily lit the yard below the bedroom window. He had spent another late night battling our neighborhood developer over a zoning change. There were thirty-one families involved, all directing questions and comments toward Ed, the civil engineer. He was putting in hours and even days researching, preparing for township boards, speaking to attorneys, and holding meetings in our home. I heard him come in through the back door. Sighing in disgust, he unrolled plat maps in the dining room, which had turned into the war room covered with boxes, stacks of petitions, and drawings. He led the fight as the principle of the matter was in the neighborhood's favor.

Hours later, crawling into bed, Ed noticed I was still awake, "Eight months have gone by. It looks as if we've hit a stale mate in the negotiations." He shifted around unable to relax.

The developer wanted something, the neighborhood

wanted something else. We were facing having to go to court and legal charges, something we did not want to do. It was in all the newspapers and Ed had been quoted a few times; it was very stressful.

"I've devoted nearly a year to this cause, and throwing in the towel is giving up. You know quitting is something I don't do," he agonized.

The following morning he alternated between strategizing in the dining room and talking to me about what to do while I dressed our youngest daughter for church. It was eating him up inside. He said firmly, "We're down to the wire and have to make a decision whether to take this to court, or withdraw from the fight. The neighborhood is counting on me."

Exasperated, I said, "Going to court means extending the process for at least a year or more. I don't think you can take this tension, our family...our marriage; it's too much."

"I hate quitting. What this guy is doing to us is wrong. It needs stopped, but you have to support me." He yelled tossing down his folder of legal paperwork.

"I know we are in the right here, Ed, but what is best for our family?" I stood facing off, "As parents, isn't the top priority to be loving and dedicated to the children and not the neighborhood? The family comes first."

"I'm doing all this for the family!" He shouted back throwing his arms out over the document laden table.

"You say you are, but are you? Is this all about a zoning change?" I blurted out grabbing our coats letting the months of frustration get to me, too.

"Don't you dare..." he said trying to cut me off.

I continued heading for the garage door. "The neighbors counting on you, the press, the pride...It's costing us something here. Can't you see that?" I slammed the door behind me.

The tension stayed high between us while driving to church. He kept making points for staying in the fight, goading me to protest, but I had nothing more to say. I was done. He knew I would back him up whatever his decision, but I hated what this was turning us into.

"I'm not going in," he snapped, pulling into the parking lot. He dropped me and the kids off at the door, barking out, "I'll be back in an hour to pick you up."

Walking into the worship center alone, I prayed for a solution. Ed later told me he drove all the way home praying for the same. Andrea and Tony turned to notice I was by myself, and I shrugged trying to hold back tears. I gave Andrea a look, the look a best friend gives when she doesn't want to talk about a fight she clearly just had with her husband. Andrea nodded. During the fourth song, I felt Ed tap me on the arm. He had come back. "Something told me to come back," he claimed, through a strained voice, neither of us aware of the other's prayer for help.

For nearly a year, we had attended Old North without missing one Sunday. Feeling the messages were so relevant in our lives, we never wanted to miss. When Brent, our pastor, stood up, I glanced at the bulletin. I could not believe how once again, he would be speaking words Ed and I needed to hear. The topic of the message was forgiveness. Dumping a can of trash out onto the alter, Pastor Brent spoke of the junk life piles at our feet. He said, "We can choose to step over the pile, even if the principle of the matter is in our favor, or mire in it and be tortured." He preached, while literally stepping over the mess; some of the papers crunching under his black shoes.

Tortured? That word spoke it all. We had spent eight

months being angry and resentful at the developer. We were trying to stop him from changing the zoning in our neighborhood out of principle, but that left us tense and stressed. Ed had lost time with the kids, and our marriage no longer seemed to be the top priority. The pastor spoke of a letting go, a walking away from the junk, as a choice. Forgiving is what we are all asking Jesus to do for us. *How can we not extend that in return?* We both sat motionless in the pew, tears rolling down our cheeks. Ed grabbed my hand and squeezed.

Leaving church just shortly after noon, my husband pulled out his cell phone and called the developer. By 4:00 the object of our rage was sitting at the very table where Andrea and I had spoken of forgiveness just days earlier. He had to have wondered why the leader of this neighborhood group, out to stop his development plans, invited him over to his house. Ed asked Tony to be there as moral support and backup. I was so proud watching Ed explain the "letting go" from the sermon at Old North and how carrying the issue any further was not worth it. The developer looked stunned as Ed extended his hand and asked for and offered forgiveness for any ill will over the past eight months.

Immediately after our unlikely guest left, my husband invited the other neighbor families over for an update. Forty plus people packed around my kitchen island as Ed explained what had transpired in his thinking and how God and forgiveness led him to the decision. Some were upset, storming out, some thought Ed had "drank the Kool-aid," but most understood. It wasn't easy for everyone to let go, but the neighbors agreed and followed his lead. Within 24 hours, an agreement was reached between the developer and the neighborhood. The weight of anger and tension dissipated freeing our family to move on.

My dining room was transformed back into a peaceful place to reminisce over the strange way the concept of forgiveness seemed to carry our family on its wings. From the quiet way it landed in a conversation with Andrea, to the moment at church when it lifted us and took us soaring into the sky, forgiveness released us from the tangle of a bitter battle. Through finding the balance, Ed and I were able to stand for what we knew was right without losing ourselves in the fight.

I was freed to see how as long as I lived clinging to the sorrows, or regrets, and even the hurts of my life; I was unable to connect with what was coming next in a positive way. In essence, I had to release the hurtful vine of yesterday before I could swing ahead to the goodness of tomorrow. In holding onto the past, I was essentially being held by the past because without realizing my part in my own rut, I gave the control to the hurt. I allowed it to control me. Once I was controlled by the pain, even if I weren't consciously focused on the past, it dictated my course by blocking me from receiving something new, something better.

The weeks following the discovery, Ed and I found new ways to communicate, accept, and forgive one another. He listened to my new understanding of God's love and the lie we both allowed to manifest in our lives, and in our marriage. Ed and I spent years trying to recover from the brutality of our early relationship. Our earnest efforts had brought us so far from those two needy people, but we still left open the file of the past so we could spend time rehashing through the nightmare as punishment on the other. It wasn't until this discovery that the files could finally be thrown away. We understood the power of God's love, the deception of sin, and how to forgive. At last, we had the whole relationship we somehow could always feel was there between the dance line girl and the swaggering frat boy with amazing good looks.

Chapter 16

Confusion: Why Isn't "It" Being Said?

Andrea

Tony and I hurried into church a few minutes late on a Sunday, which Kimberly thought was funny because the contemporary service didn't start until 11:00 am. She'd once teased, "It's practically a weekly lunch appointment." Leaning past Ed, she pretended to scold, glancing at her watch. Tony smiled sarcastically at her, and then, we turned our focus to the worship. A guest was invited to share, so the congregation was quietly seated. I listened intently as the principal of a Christian school spoke to us about their sports program and curriculum. He described the importance of achieving higher test scores and out-playing the public schools on the fields and courses. With excitement he reported how they had to reach higher because they were representing Jesus to the world. I wondered if the Christian organizations, whose job it was to relieve individuals from the endless struggles, were in fact pressuring them to strive on *in the name of Jesus.*

The Christian school principal was kind and obviously passionate about his position, feeling it was more than a job; it was his ministry. I was sorry he believed in and promoted the ladder, though. It was clear he knew Jesus was the Son of God and His name should be glorified; in fact, he said it was more important to bring glory to God than to do anything else. He just thought God was glorified when his group of kids proved themselves by out testing and out winning.

Considering competition, I felt we could still compete to the best of our abilities, trying to win; and we could still encourage high test scores, but not as our way of showing our worth or the validity of our message. It seemed an odd distinction, the difference between achieving ones best for the purpose of being who God intended, and striving for a measure of personal glory to fill a need.

On the ride home, Tony listened to my concerns, "The message stands on its own," I insisted. "The *Bible* is clear; it is by our *love* that the world will know we are Christians. Love growing naturally out of the knowledge of the truth the way fruit grows from a tree."

Tony questioned, "It's clear that some people are gifted to run faster than others or are impressively athletic, and so it would be less than God intended if they failed to tap into their potential, right?"

"Yes," I admitted, "and the same concept would hold true for academics, art, music, or whatever. It would be a shame to imply that excellence is wrong because some people possess more ability than others. Those who are not gifted in athletic ways or academic ways should seek out the nature of their own talents and excel in those areas, rather than insisting that no one have the opportunity to display athletic or academic quality."

We agreed, but as we talked over what the principle actually said, there was an implication that the game and test scores carried weight to make God look good. When he alluded to the school's need for superiority, I understood the difference between selling the institution as competitive and an attempt at validating their Heavenly stamp of approval. It was the difference between achieving greatness and feeling validated by it.

Tony drove the rest of the way home silently, while I thought about how fruit draws upon the inner health and strength of the plant from which it springs. "If the principal focused his attention on showing Christ to the world through the freedom and vitality of the students, instead of the hope of being better at climbing for the glory prize; the students would have what they need to be different. They would have the stock to produce something the world is literally dying to find." Tony patted my hand. Lacing his fingers with mine, and admitted, "I never saw it that way before."

Kimberly

Ed and I had a Mexican lunch ritual following church, so we could discuss the message over a basket of chips and salsa. While enjoying the aromas of fresh tomatoes, spicy meat, and fried tortillas, I said, "Andrea and I have been saying almost the opposite of what the man said today." Unfolding the napkin onto my lap, I persisted, "I mean, those Christian kids could be internalizing the wrong message. It's scary."

Ed asked, "So what if those kids are thinking they have to out shine the 'non-Christians' to be great for Jesus? What's the big deal?" Ed always had a way of bringing things down to Earth, but this time, he was missing my point.

"Think about it," I said directly, "setting Christian kids on some proverbial ladder will leave them with the impression of having to judge others, assessing the value of their peers to compare with their own. It will also give nonbelievers the view of Christians as judgmental and self-righteous. What we once thought!" He nodded letting me continue. "If Jesus came to save us from the emptiness of not good enough, then we don't need to force our way past someone to step up higher, as we will be living free lives full of purpose and good intent. That's what people are looking for, the freedom to live fulfilled. Trying to show the world we are better is a reflection of the message gone awry."

Ed grabbed my hand across the table, "You are really on to something here; this could change people's lives. It's beautiful." I knew he was sincere and not just trying to make feel better. I knew because the message changed us.

Andrea

Sitting in church listening about the love of Jesus or building on the foundation was comforting. I wondered, though, if there were people in the congregation thinking they were building on the foundation, but leaving each week with nothing more than a renewed sense of trying harder to be better Christians. Knowing I was once that way myself, I thought about our pastor and hoped he knew some of the people didn't understand. I wanted the world of Christianity to know, some of the people are buckling under the burden of the morality of our faith, eating the apple of trying to live up to God.

Sunday nights involved small group, and Kimberly and I pulled into the driveway of our small group leader's home at the same time. Ed helped Tony carry in bags of chips and drinks. I asked Kimberly as we walked up to the door, "Why isn't 'it' being said? Beyond 'Jesus saves' and 'Jesus gives eternal life' there is no explanation of worth or value coming from God. I have been in church since I was six-years-old, but I had to learn it in my kitchen with you. Finding the whole truth of the message took digging and searching."

"Maybe we missed that week," Kimberly joked. I recognized her reference to our lady friend at the welcome dinner. We laughed, but neither of us was sure of the answer.

"I'm going to ask the small group to give me the gospel message as if I were hearing it for the first time," I told Kimberly in defiance.

"Are you sure you want to know," she smirked, "we may realize we are alone in our beliefs..."

After being asked, each very faithful, God-loving small group member said Jesus would save us from Hell and give us eternal life if we would believe in Him. I didn't disagree with what they said except to note it wasn't really the whole message. And I knew if a Christian embarked upon the journey armed with less than the full message, they could likely end up further from God than when they started.

Kimberly

I loved being a part of a small group at Old North. Andrea had said yes for me and Ed before she even asked us, and I wasn't sure what she had committed us to do. By our second meeting, we were hooked. The people were not just friendly but knowledgeable. Ed loved hearing the scriptural references, and Andrea and I loved challenging the group with deep Biblical questions. Sometimes, I think we came off a little strong. Maybe… just maybe, asking them point blank to give us the full message of Christ was one of those nights.

After hearing the message from our Christian small group friends, I tried to come to some understanding. Nothing said answered the question of why we sin. *Where was the notion of living fully Jesus referred to in His sermons? Were we all painted into the doctrinal corner of waiting for paradise?* I was confused as to why the feelings of valuelessness or unworthiness were not being explained in churches to underscore why we sin. Occasionally, the devil had been blamed for temptation, mostly in one on one conversation with church members. Even then, evil could only prevail in the life of a person who had no understanding of how to love, or how God's great love gives them value, worth, purpose. Without understanding the whole message, how could any of us ever change? Maybe that was why so many of us never do.

Andrea

Tony knew I was frustrated with the patented delivery of the message we had heard our whole lives. He had also grown up in a Christian home and attended church and Christian school. On the way home from small group, I sorted through what was bothering me, "As believers, we denounce each act of sin separately, and condemn falling short without offering an explanation for why we do it or what makes it all equal in God's eyes." I preached on about how we pick the endless task of debating the results of individual choices rather than carrying on the message, which heals the wound. Going after the disease would end the cyclical pattern of symptoms, the destructive choices we are constantly trying to stop. It seemed ridiculous.

I started to press, "We never explain *how* the blood frees us." Turning to face him, I asked, "Did anyone ever tell you *how* you would be free? Did someone sit down and teach you anything beyond the list of dos and don'ts?"

He shook his head, signaling surrender and admitted, "As far as sin, no. No one ever said why I do it. Just giving into temptation, I guess." He paused and then offered a rare comment, "I mostly try to live a clean life and serve others to show Jesus to the world."

I knew, by most churches standards, Tony would have been awarded a badge for spouse of the year. It made me sad to think he felt he had to live a cleaner life because I could see his tendency was to try to live a "perfect" life. It was difficult to see the sin in his choice of living. He was straining to hold up the wooden board of best husband, good Christian, and strong father. I knew he could identify sin when it was clearly wrong, but I also knew identifying the sin of trying too hard to be a "good person" was almost impossible to do. In the same way I always had, he overlooked or treated the symptoms and ignored the disease. He had never seriously addressed what caused something to be sinful or how his perfect image could be a sin.

I tried to stop thinking aloud but heard myself saying, "The Christian authorities often fail to explain there is more to salvation than hanging on by a thread until it's our turn to go to heaven." I wanted Tony to know we should not be waiting for paradise as much as preparing for it, by living now, as who we were created to be. "In this way, it's about me. This life is about me because I will give an account to God for how I spent my money and my time, how I raised my family, and what I did with the knowledge of Jesus Christ." He was stunned to hear me say something was about me; he was dialed in for the conclusion. I gave him my new version of love thy neighbor, "I can't see others as having limitless value and serve them out of love until I adopt this perspective of myself. Otherwise, the serving or giving is done in a selfish attempt to gain approval from God or to feel value or purpose for myself instead of out of love for the other person."

Kimberly

We had already discussed the tendency of faithful believers to wait for God to come along and poof their lives into shape, and I'd encountered a few "Super Christians" who let others know how much *Bible* knowledge they have, or how many verses they could recite, or even how much they volunteered at the church. Too holy to really associate with any other group of people except those they had deemed appropriate for their holiness, they ranked sins and attached eternal predictions based on the rankings. They don't have the entire message as they keep attaining the next Christian rung or re-painting the front of their cut-out, trying to find worth in God's eyes.

A new church member may have just given their heart to follow Jesus but cannot seem to stop the constant destructive behaviors. They could gauze away the pain of the need by drinking, shopping, or having an affair because inside, they are looking for value. I knew a complete agnostic or even atheist may never turn to find

God because the Christians they know keep outwardly sinning or passing judgment. They don't want any part of becoming that critical or part of a God system that is ok with such judgment.

A few silent minutes into the ride, I finally blurted to Ed, "No-one says people sin because of an inner belief telling us we are not of value or have no worth." I barely paused to breathe, "It's that unworthiness feeling of not being good enough, which leads to the searching, Christian or not. The sin is in the search!" Ed listened, wrinkling up his forehead as I continued, "Without God, we would be nothing, but that should not be confused with we *are* nothing. When we understand that Jesus' love completes us and gives us our value from the moment we were conceived, maybe even before, we will no longer be dominated by the endless searching for value and worth through other things, in other words: sinning."

It may have sounded as if we were re-defining sin, a scary proposition for two women in rural Ohio, but it was more a clarification for what had always been. The apple concept was a way to view the traditional sin story from a practical viewpoint. It was the explanation behind the endless drive to sin and the inability in us all to change. It was the definition of sin nature.

Ed stayed silent pondering the deep statements of faith I was trying to expound upon. I was wound up, "People all around us are dying spiritually, Ed. Couples aren't staying married, over 85% of recovering drug addicts relapse, and teens are starving themselves or joining gangs and engaging in dangerous lifestyles. They are dropping out of school by the thousands every year, and one in three middle class working Americans are on some kind of mood stabilizing pharmaceutical." He kept shaking his head, as I kept shaking. "Why isn't it being said?" I cried.

Jesus gave eternal life to the souls whose faith is in His love. He died to pay for our sins and prove our value, so we could be free and abundant and full. He did not die for worthless people but for the generous love of the people He created. He wanted each of us, as His unique creations, to live fully into His specific designs. The image perfectly designed to be free from want, status, or approval, free from believing the lie of not enough. The image perfectly designed to become fruits of *His Spirit*. In believing we have worth and are loved, we are transformed, beyond measure to live into completeness. It is good news.

Andrea

We were too awake to go right into our houses; so once arriving home, Kimberly and I took an evening walk through Westbury Park. We talked about how people were walking into church looking for answers and how each of us had once gone to church looking for God, wanting to find explanations for our questions. One of us left unimpressed, and the other stayed laboring under the false idea of running a mini PR campaign for God. We both ended up empty and unfulfilled.

In frustration, I huffed, "If churches would share *how* Jesus fills us up… If they would say, 'His desire is to awaken the soul we deny, the soul He designed for us to express… then, the majority of believers would actually be armed with real Good News to share instead of the arduous job of selling real estate in Heaven or scaring people into salvation with a vivid enough description of Hell."

Kimberly didn't respond to my accusation, but instead asked, "Do you remember that pastor we heard; the one who went as far as to lament the difficulty of tempting non-Christian Americans with the promise of Heaven?" She knew I remembered; how could I forget? He was so earnest, saying, "It's easier to do missionary evangelism in foreign countries because heaven sounds too good to pass up to people in poorer countries."

I sighed, knowing there was a better way, I urged, "The system closes around you. You're so grateful to God for the promise of eternal life, that once you believe He sent His Son to die for you, it feels ungrateful to admit that your still wondering everyday why it's so hard to love or feel joy." I thought of the times I'd beat myself up for not having the fruit of the spirit, the patience, the self-control, as if I could force it to appear by performing acts of love and smiling when I was actually dying inside.

Kimberly agreed, "Without the whole message, we are simply replacing our sinful way of living with a sinful way of living under the heading of Christianity."

Kimberly

It was curious to be experiencing the familiar concerns *as a Christian*, because as a once, questioning non-believer, I could sense this lack of genuineness a mile away. I could smell it, taste it, and even feel it whenever I was around a "Super Christian." It was part of my excuse to stay away. I saw the tally in their minds racking up the inappropriateness of my conversation or my lifestyle. They weren't genuine, and at times, I felt even feared me, as if I could rub off some sin or something on them. Explaining it to Andrea, I said, "I know scripture can be tilted in the direction to appear supportive of this type of judgment; however, the predominate theme in the New Testament is love." I advised, "If we understand one day we will come face to face with who we were without the Earthly crutches of an admiring social circle, misinterpreted scriptures, or even an approving congregation then we must know our testimony will certainly be more about how we loved than judged." I knew that if we wanted to wonder why it was so hard to bring a nonbeliever into church, it would not be a bad idea to first look in the mirror.

"You're right," Andrea endorsed, "it's as if we study every verse in the *Bible* but miss the overall message of the chapter or book."

Andrea

The following weeks were spent taking that long look in the mirror. It was excruciating. I considered the way I'd hammered home the idea that the Ten Commandments were a healthier way to live, and "doing it God's way" was right because He said so. I taught my children they would benefit from following God's rules, please Him with their obedience, and thus, show other people His light. This was morality, not faith. I was teaching the necessity of living the results of the discovery without making sure those I taught had actually been awakened. It was worse than putting the cart before the horse. It was hitching the cart to *them* without telling them there was a horse. *Faith is something*, I thought, *and while morality can mimic faith, even be birthed from it, it is not the faith itself.*

E-ing:

Why It's Important

in L.I.F.E.

Andrea

Jesus promised to give rest to those who brought the weight of their lives to Him. Once I understood how insurmountable the black hole of my feeling of spiritual debt was, I could see how it sucked in and absorbed everything I thought, hoped, and even achieved. Only then could I fully grasp, by accepting that I owed nothing; through no act of my own, Jesus was bringing me to a zero balance. He brought me to a level place where I could actually build into His original plan for my life. Instead of being overcome by emptiness, I could be full enough to spill into the lives of others around me. I simply needed to find the right words to communicate my faith.

Kimberly

I was in California at a meeting for work, and I spent the allotted bit of free time in a little seaport market strolling along, listening to the harbor sounds. I saw a refrigerator magnet in one of the souvenir shops where I was browsing. It read, "I've spent the first half of my life getting abused by my parents and the second half by my kids." I thought, *That pretty much sums it up for me.* But what if living in a broken world had more to do with acceptance than blame? After all, if I were going to assign a reason for everyone who had ever gauzed onto me, which I needed to do, I should also try to figure out how to deal with the understanding not everyone turns to God to fill the void. Sitting on the harbor watching sailboats glide by, I thought, *If we were all broken, then the only solution I can come to is to love.* Since I had learned my value, I knew there was a way to love, which wouldn't allow people to ever hurt me, but that would hope, pray, and believe that one day they would find peace in their hearts. I wanted to extend it to telling others about the love of Jesus, but if someone would have spoken that way to me, I would have slammed the door in their face. Looking back, my hesitance, my questions, my self-righteousness stemmed from my separateness from God in the first place. How could anyone ever have told me that?

Our business dinner meeting was being served at a beautiful restaurant late in the evening. One of my colleagues met me in the lobby and asked if I wanted to have a drink in the hotel bar while we waited for the rest of our group.

I ordered a diet coke, which looked meager next to

her pink cosmopolitan. Squeezing the lime into the glass, she batted her eyes mockingly and asked, "Are you ready for what I'm about to say?" Barely pausing to allow an answer, she divulged a story she'd been dying to tell. She was recently divorced and elated to be out in the world again having fun. "Kimberly," she patted my hand, "I'm making up for lost time."

Her eyes lit up telling me of a new guy she'd met a few months prior and how the chemistry between them was amazing. She went on and on about how he was a pilot and even though he lived five states away, he would fly in to see her at least every couple of weeks. They had long rendezvous in his hotel room, and she told me explicit things he did to please her. We giggled and laughed as she continued along. She was so in to her story, and even showed me pictures he had sent on her phone; they were graphic enough to prompt me to politely ask her to stop. The entire time though, I listened. Since she was mid-thirties and he looked to be also, I asked, "So what's his deal…divorced? Never married?"

With aloofness she replied, "He's married, but he was going to leave his wife. She got pregnant, though. So, he's still married, but he's NEVER home and it's not really good…" She trailed off sensing my shock, and then added, "I try not to think of that, though, I'm just having fun and thinking about him with a family makes it way too personal."

My stomach flipped, lurching as I wanted to hug her and slap her face to try to wake her up. In my head I screamed, *You're worth so much more than that!* Tears welled in my eyes, but before they could fall, I excused myself to the bathroom. My awakened life brimmed with emotion for her. Love, compassion, strength, I wanted to pour them into the pink cosmo, but I knew she wouldn't accept them, that flavor unfamiliar. She needed more than I could provide. Thankfully when I returned, the rest of our party was ready to leave for dinner. I avoided her the rest of the night because I knew what to say, but couldn't. She needed so much that she was willing to give herself up to someone who clearly was using her, and it was going to lead no where. *It always leads no where.*

I laid awake on my hotel bed telling myself to accept where she was on her journey of life without judgment. *She's abundantly loved as much as I am, as much as we all are, yet she can't feel it,* I reminded myself. I knew one day the pilot would stop needing her or he'd cease to be enough of a gauze to make her feel loved. Either way, I knew it would one day come to an end, probably in frustration and hurt. What I didn't know was how to sit by and watch.

Rolling over to see it was 4:00 a.m., I realized it was 7:00 in Ohio. *Andrea is up now,* I thought, *I'm calling her.* As soon as she answered, I told her the story. I was sick to my stomach and furious, "I can't ride in on a white horse and save her!" I screamed into the phone, "What are we supposed to do?" She acknowledged not knowing, and I persisted, "Watching the precision with which other people gauze away or climb up is so keen, Andrea! It's a cinematic front row seat to a show I don't want to see."

"You missed a chance to tell her she didn't have to give herself away in order to feel alive; it would have been the greatest gift," Andrea started without considering the implications.

"What was I supposed to say?" I demanded.

"How about, do you have a few hours to learn about the way we sin, and why?" She tried to lighten the mood, but we both knew it wasn't that simple.

"The battle facing me now is deciding if I should share the amazing power of soul value that God's love has shown me, or just stay quiet," I admitted. "To some people, I want to shout it from the rooftops, but I know if I do, they will close down. No one wants the message, but we all need it. We all are searching for it..."

Andrea

After considering the ways I would try to explain the apple concept to another person, I fumed, "It's so frustrating having my eyes opened and having no untainted words to express the truth that's changing me. All the words have been dirtied up or have lost their luster. Nothing means what I'm saying." I protested, "When you say 'I'm a Christian' people picture whatever awful idea they already have or maybe even imagine you as their grandmother was." At some point in history the word grace meant a wealth of beautiful things. It spoke of unmerited favor and love, giving the idea of being scooped up and saved. "Saved," I said, "Now there's a word that's received with delight. Can you imagine how it feels to hear someone say, 'You need to be saved'," I asked, though I felt as if I had been.

Kimberly

I finally answered, knowing I was saved from the way I'd once lived, "Saying, 'you need to be saved' is offensive. It feels like such an insult." I knew I couldn't help someone who wasn't asking for it, and I couldn't push my beliefs onto another. "We just have to talk about the joy, peace, and patience we're experiencing," I suggested.

"Yeah," Andrea answered sarcastically, "to Christians, we're simply listing the fruit of the spirit. To non-Christians, we'll just sound like fruits."

Laughing, I breathed a sigh of acceptance, "We *do* sound like fruits."

Andrea

I told her in seriousness, "It isn't a joke at all when I am looking into the face of someone I really care about, hearing her say some of the same things that once kept me awake at night." I concluded, "A real feeling of fear comes over me, and I'm afraid to say what I'm thinking. It's easier to sit by and listen."

Kimberly was right with me, "Well, I don't want to be predictable and preachy. I don't want to act like I have the answers. Who am I to be so bold?" We knew there was not a formula we could hand to a person to make it all clear.

"I guess, if we're going to be faced with people who hold differing opinions or pose doubts in the form of questions, we'll have to remember what a process it was for us," I decided.

Shrugging to myself, I added, "I have to be comfortable enough within myself to talk about my point-of-view from personal conviction, not with a goal of helping or changing someone else." I knew I had to be open to learn from others, respecting them enough not to try to make them believe what I believed. We said good bye, knowing we'd see each other soon. "Have a nice flight home," I wished.

"See ya, tomorrow."

Hanging up, I felt compelled; E-ing was the most important thing I could do. Remembering back to the evangelism sermon at Old North, I wondered how I could articulate what I was dying to say. One hope entered my mind, *As I lift up the cup of salvation and drink freely from it, my liberties will say the words which are escaping me.* Certainly at times to Christians I would seem to be sinning, and to non-Christians I would seem like a Jesus freak.

Early the following morning, Kimberly sat quietly at my counter recovering from jet lag as I pre-heated the oven to make some biscuits. Lisa, a good friend of ours, was stopping by for breakfast. She came in late, explaining her tardiness was due to rummage sale-ing. Looking at her in her Birkenstocks, I considered how I'd never felt stupid or embarrassed in front of her. She liked me even though she thought Christians to be a little off. I'd learned a lot from listening to her talk about politics and philosophy.

As we commenced our visit, she began telling Kimberly and me how she was in the process of redoing her bathroom. Sharing her idea with us, she enthusiastically asked, "Have you seen the magnetic poetry?" We nodded as she continued, "I'm going to use epoxy to stick it to the walls. I also want to have a board with loose words so people can *sit* and make poems of their own." Kimberly and I were both more traditional and predictable in our decorating than Lisa, so while she shared her vision, there were some awkward moments of silence, and I think I said, "humm, ok," a few times. She gave some examples of the poems she was considering before changing the subject. She told us how some of her other friends had sent her a copy of a popular book which said each person was created with one single purpose, to please God.

"I believe we *are* created for His pleasure," I said, "but the expectation has to be coupled with an awareness of what pleases God."

With the idea for her bathroom in mind, I said, "What if God sees you remodeling your bathroom, and He is pleased and thrilled because no one else on the planet would ever epoxy magnetic poetry to the walls as decor? What if you are fulfilling your purpose perfectly when you are being you, doing what you do without worrying who it will impress?" She sat facing me without speaking; I went on, "What if God is pointing at you in that bathroom and reading the poems you're gluing to the walls and loving you?" I almost cried. I loved the idea of the magnetic poetry for the first time too because it was one example of what made Lisa so special.

I got choked up because she had made it clear she didn't consider herself a Christian, but in this way, she was closer to following the lead of Jesus than most of the people I'd encountered in a lifetime of church. She didn't wear an image like a mask but showed herself to the world without pretense. She didn't compare herself with others to build herself up. Her light shined and pointing that out was a way to fan the flame in her, while teaching me to live fully, too.

Kimberly

I was glad we weren't trying to "save" Lisa; she would have known it in a second. I couldn't wave a magic wand and make it all make sense. I couldn't explain what had transformed in me without sounding crazy, but Lisa had been with us and knew how we felt. She was being herself and allowing us to do the same.

Joking, later that day on the phone, I said, "God made the world beautiful, but we're not tulips." Everywhere I looked, the identical appearance of the popular flowers seemed to be an expression of the opposite of our discovery. If He wanted us all to be oblivious and alike we would just be tulips. I knew God wanted more for us than that. He intended for us to experience life, to live it fully. We are not automatic or inert, but rather thinking, emotional, sinful, beautiful God created creatures that have a chance at something wonderful in this life.

"Andrea, if we could just have been handed a manual, a guide from God to teach us the steps. People are so lost and confused. I was, but if we had a manual we could read it and know what to do, how to love, how to give." She laughed as I bantered on about wanting a manual from God, until the words struck me; I exploded in laughter. "A manual! God should give us a Manuel so we can understand," I screamed into the phone.

"I'd buy it," she responded playing along.

"No, listen to the words, a manual, say them out loud," I urged, "We need ...a...man...u...al...." The phone went silent on the other end, as she figured out the play on words. I finished, "God DID give us a manual... Emmanuel!"

"You are so ridiculous," Andrea laughed.

"I don't care. I'll never go back. You can't make me."

"Me neither...I don't want to go back," Andrea agreed.

The love that follows an experience of freedom, with its silliness and bliss, is the dream come true of a once buried soul, a soul that got a second chance to live.

I walked around for days looking at the world so alive and grateful for it all: the buds on the trees, my family, the hopes and dreams I still held close. The new world I was experiencing was beautiful and in pain at the same time. Dealing with both sides to life had overwhelming moments, but I wanted to start doing something. I had to start living out what I'd learned and sharing deep conversations with Ed and Andrea were no longer enough of a change. Involving my family was part of the process.

I wanted to teach my daughters they could give back to our beautiful world in everyday circumstances. In the same ways that Lisa shared herself, we could all do the equivalent through random acts of kindness.

On one of our special mall outings, we were sitting at dinner, and all three of my daughters were chatting up which stores they wanted to shop. I realized it was a moment I could use to teach them the world is a lot more fun if we gave back to it rather than when we focused on our own wants and needs. I gave them a challenge. Each daughter, ages four, eight, and twelve would have to give one random act of kindness before leaving the mall. If completed, the reward would be dessert, which we were going to skip until the end of the evening. I looked down at three wrinkled foreheads on faces with perplexed expressions. There was only one rule; they couldn't ask me for help in any way, not even with ideas. They had to think of the gesture and act it out all by themselves. It was interesting to see who attempted first, second, and third. I realized when the baby, then middle, and finally, the oldest daughter performed a kind act that as we age, we hesitate in doing nice things for people. Through our embarrassment, rushed lives, or melancholy existences, we forget how we all need each other.

My youngest helped the custodian pick up some trash from the floor, my middle daughter helped the restaurant woman clear trays, and my oldest helped a small child down the slide in the recreation area. They were as proud of themselves as I was of them. They gleefully announced what dessert they were going to pick as we started out of the mall into the food court. True to form, my middle daughter shouted, "But mommy you didn't do yours!"

She got me on that one. "Oh, of course," I said, forcing

a smile. "I am going to do mine right now." I searched for something I could do that would look kind to my girls but would require the least amount of embarrassment as possible. I thought of the ice cream line, *Whoever is in front of us in line, I will pay for their dessert.*

In line, the only person ahead of us was a gentleman I guessed to be in his mid 80's. He ordered a banana split and started to reach into his pocket to pay the $2.83. I jumped in front of him with my arm waving three one-dollar bills and announced, "I'll be paying for you today." The cashier froze not knowing whose money to take. The two teenage boys standing behind me in line looked uncomfortable, darting their eyes down when I caught their stunned expressions. The elderly man slowly turned to me taking a gaited step back. He uttered a bit bewildered, "But... I don't know you."

Wrapping my arms around my girls squeezing them into a small huddle, I smiled, "I know you don't, but I am trying to teach my daughters how to show kindness in the world, and today, we chose you."

He stood up straight, turned toward me and wiped his mouth with a handkerchief. "Well let me tell you something," he said in a shaky whisper, "I am having a hard time talking. I have throat cancer, and I do not have much longer to live." He paused to clear his throat wiping his mouth again, "but once I get to heaven I am going to tell them what you did for me." My eyes welled. I was speechless. Looking down at my girls, I noticed they were glossy eyed too. Everyone was; the cashier, the man, even the teenage boys looked moved. My daughters experienced the best lesson I could have hoped for, and I affirmed the need to give of myself more often in love.

I thanked him for graciously allowing me to pay, and he

said he should be the one saying thanks, but I knew better. A few solemn minutes past as the girls and I ordered our own desserts still shaken from the encounter. Walking out the door, we passed by him. As we waved and called out good-bye, he simply smiled under a spoonful of vanilla and pointed up to the sky.

Chapter 18

Reflecting: Avoiding the Potholes

Andrea

The living room of my parent's condo was beautifully decorated with items long packed away. My mom had constructed a personal history museum, using pieces of our past from every one of the homes we'd lived in. Flipping on the ceiling fan to cool the room, she declared, "I'm starting over with all of my favorite stuff! I don't care if it's "in" or not; I want my memories in full view."

Surrounded by the things which represented my life, it struck me that it was her life, as well. Glancing at my mother, I wondered how hard it must have been to be a young wife; a mother to four small children, when she was sick for so long. I thought about how many times we'd stood side-by-side at her stove or mine making delicious food or sat together studying our *Bibles*. My mom was such an amazing woman, and waking up, I realized she was just someone's daughter, too, who grew up to face so many obstacles: a wrong idea of what was expected from a wife, a horrible illness, a legal nightmare, and Houdini friends who all disappeared. When my parents reached out to God for help, they mistakenly grabbed the hand of a broken leader instead; they fell for the "bad jesus." Trying to live into who they thought God expected them to be, my mom and dad gave us their very best.

I was impressed with my parents; they endured, teaching us some amazing lessons in the process. We learned restraint and commitment; they passed on their passion for family and a remarkable ability to endure hardships while remaining constant. My dad never missed a day's work in thirty years, providing for our every physical need. He told me he loved me every day, and even when we lived in the same house, he wrote me letters when I needed encouragement. He taught me that justice would prevail, and good could come from even the worst times in my life if I focused on what was important. The generosity shown to us growing up spilled out into our lives and could be passed on to our children, too, only I'd be adding the rest of the message.

"What are you thinking about?" My mom asked.

"Tell me about your life," I answered.

So, with her legs crossed and her mug placed neatly on a napkin in front of her, she sat telling me familiar stories about how her own mother raised her to be a dutiful wife and homemaker, the apple she was fed.

Kimberly

My father could not supply me all of what I needed, but I chased after it anyway. My father's father, his father, and his father before that had the same problem, but like a greyhound chasing a rabbit around the track, it was never going to happen, because it wasn't supposed to. There was no one capable of providing the completeness within us except Our Heavenly Father. Trying to extrude it out of another person was unfair to them. Once we understood the fullness of His love, we could stop running, stop chasing after what we could not attain. Focused on the absolute love from God within ourselves, we could then love others unstinted, too.

My mom and dad had carried on the Sunday dinner tradition started when I was a child at my grandparents. Every week, my brother, sister, and I each came with our spouses and kids to pile into the home where we were raised. We usually didn't discuss deep or personal issues, but I decided to step out of my comfort zone and ask my father what he thought he passed on to me as his daughter. It was a warm day so we ate outside on the concrete patio. Waiting at the picnic table for the serving dish, he responded with a joke about passing on a love for the Cleveland Indians. However, he quickly learned this was one day I was going to be serious. Without looking over at me, he took a minute to think about his answer, I could see him retrieving the words, as if I'd asked for a map he knew one day I'd request.

Slowly nodding his head, he began, "I hope first you learned how to love."

I watched him sitting there knowing I had learned to love in the truest way.

"Compassion," he stated simply, "Compassion."

I had always felt empathy and had a strong degree of compassion. Listening to him, I thought about God's love and how I saw everyone as infinite and valuable and loved, knowing it was compassion in the purest form.

He finished, after a long pause, "We wanted you to have some sense of spirituality."

Again, I could say he had passed on a sense of spirituality to me, as well. It was interesting how this man who rarely displayed an emotional side hoped I learned three things *of the heart* from him, and I had. He taught me all of those things and more.

Taking off his ball cap, he rubbed his forehead, "You know, I did the best I could. I knew I was going to make some mistakes, but I really tried."

I watched my parents interact with the family the rest of the afternoon. They weren't aware, but I saw each of them for the first time in my life as children of God themselves, as lights intended to shine in full illumination. My mother was so diligent in making sure we all had enough food, fun, whatever. My dad was so engulfed in the latest sports statistics or baseball score. The momentary glance they gave each other saying with their eyes, *we're not that bad; look what we made.* But on this day, at that moment, I saw something more behind those surface roles they both maintained for years. I saw joy and contentment. They wanted nothing more in life than that Sunday afternoon surrounded with their grown children all living good lives and grandchildren who were spoiled rotten by love.

As I was loading the last of the kids into the car to leave, my dad told me, "I think I am the luckiest man in the world to have my health, your mom, and this family." Despite everything I'd learned from my father, nothing inspired me more than observing his ability to stay grounded; his knowing how to prioritize what was really important.

His own wound blinded him to the impact his harsh words left on me during my youth. Trying to prove him wrong or attempting to stop the pain caused by the misleading notion of what he meant, I made some poor choices, but they were my choices. I had no anger for my father, only love. The family needed to provide an image he wanted to have in his mind that quieted the little voice saying *he* wasn't enough. When I differed from that image, it reminded him of what *he thought* he wasn't. Putting the pressure on me, he tried to force me to be better, do better, and know better. I saw that and understood his need behind those words. I hoped he would learn, even in his 60's, because Jesus had died for him; he was enough, too.

It was early evening when we pulled back into our driveway, and I noticed Andrea out on the porch with Tony. They were laughing at the kids out in the yard playing with their new black puppy. "Ed," I said, turning to him as he parked the car, "Let's walk over." He told the kids they could play for a minute while we said hello. Putting the leash on our dog, I told her she could come over with us to meet the fuzzy, little puppy.

The men started in on sports talk and statistics, so we meandered into the grass where we could escape the information on batting averages and designated hitters. Watching our two husbands, who now were co-coaches and small group friends, who had taken to planning events together without us, was remarkable and funny.

As we settled under the tree in the front yard, I acknowledged, "Our friendship was enough of a gift, but to have our husbands become friends...well, that's just ridiculous."

"It's too much," Andrea beamed. "How was your family today?" she asked, knowing I'd just come from seeing my parents.

"Fine. Great, as usual," I answered, not immediately certain I would talk about my conversation with my dad as if I wanted to keep the beautiful picture of him in my mind all to myself.

"What else?" she asked, sensing I was holding back, "Can you talk about it?"

"Well," I started, "Today just really solidified for me how believing the lie took me away from the person I was intended to be on yet another level. It robbed me of enjoying wonderful moments with family, seeing people as *they* were intended to be." Andrea stood with her hands in her pockets, staring at the dogs and nodding her approval as I explained, "I am amazed how I catch the joy in every moment, every interaction. I'm so grateful for my mom, dad, sister, brother and loving them by just watching them live. It's nice."

My ability to feel for others was stunted because I had so desperately tended to my own wound. I knew there were degrees to this, and I may have been a decent, caring person, but my love was inadvertently held back by my own need for worth throughout life. The need for value within us blocks us from authentically knowing the people who share our lives. It becomes the filter through which all of our relationships are then sieved gumming up a barrier between us and the people we love.

With the barrier washed away that kept me at arms length from my family; that kept me from the closeness of real love and friendship, I was now exposed to the raw and organic love for others.

On the long drive home from my parents, I had

lamented through thoughts of individuals with huge deep voids left from physical and emotional scars of abusive or absent parents, circumstances too unfathomable to discuss. Explaining to Andrea, I realized how difficult it must be to love others, grow and mature into responsible adults, or even care about one's own children if the wound is deep enough; if they never uncover the lie they'd been forced to believe. The barrier still stands as they wander around seeking worth and love. It's deep, subconscious, but so invasive that it affects everything if it goes unrecognized. People end up really hurting themselves and others in the process of seeking to fill that need.

I could recall the names and faces of the children on my former caseload, as a social worker. Forced from their abusive homes to live with strangers, they never knew they were loved. Too often, they were expelled from school, labeled as having behavioral problems, and made to endure countless medical and psychological appointments. Some of them ended up making poor enough choices to end up in juvenile detention centers where the numbers reach into the hundreds of thousands. All were children of worthlessness, oblivious to their immense value from God; I was disgusted. I knew how encompassing, how permeating the wound of not enough was in my own life. *It has to be for everyone,* I thought, knowing, to really love and serve others, this had to be recognized and restored.

I allowed myself to momentarily imagine how I would now be more equipped to help them break the heart-wrenching cycle of abuse and abandonment. The task of communicating love to those children humbled me and moved me to tears.

Andrea

Leaning against the tree in my front yard, I suggested, "I guess the starting point can be a specific event or even a more subtle insinuation. A person who suffered unspeakable physical or mental abuse has an obvious wound, while a life of general worthlessness is an existence that spreads a person thin over time. Essentially, the apple can be jammed down your throat or fed to you slowly, one bite here, one bite there."

"Yes, I'd say so," Kimberly agreed, adding, "The important thing is to find your place of brokenness or the way in which you are broken, not to blame, but to heal."

I knew Kimberly was right because I could go back to the day a man molested me in the same room with my family, who then did nothing about it, but that didn't explain how I became a girl who would sit through it quietly and wait to tell anyone it happened. I couldn't pinpoint the moment I started believing my value came from keeping the "peace" or trying to be a "perfect" person. I could only identify it as a life long tendency reinforced by my experiences growing up.

"What are you thinking about?" Kimberly asked, leaning into my line of vision.

Without making eye contact, I answered, "The problem comes in trying to directly correlate the life experience with the need. I mean the length to which certain people go to feel fulfilled or the degree to which they feel a void is not always in proportion with the pain they experienced in life."

Kimberly agreed, "You can't measure what someone has felt because the reactions or desperate choices to find value will also reflect a personality or temperament. Then, there is the problem of carrying that wound into our adult lives." She gave a wave to Ed letting him know it was time to leave. Turning, she added, "We never really understand how we're festering in worthlessness." I watched as they walked home arm-in-arm with their children and dog in tow.

What Kimberly had said was true. Tony and I carried on in brokenness when we felt insecure about ourselves or unsure of decisions we were making for our children. We threw our childhoods and the ways we were raised in each other's faces pointing to them as reasons the other was inadequate as a parent. We insulted our pasts without knowing those personal histories were valuable pieces of a picture we needed to be complete, not only as parents, but also as people. Those pasts could have provided us with vital clues into understanding how we were tempted by the apple we were each fed and the ways we chose to remedy the void left after taking bites. Instead, we were convinced it was a contest and one of us would emerge as the boss of our kids and the other just a follower. The winner would make decisions and be respected; the loser would just be a loser. But we were changed, we had the doors blown off of our lives when we came to Westbury, and although it had its uncomfortable moments, we were better for it.

I sent the kids into the house, and Tony scooped up the tiny puppy. Carrying her over to me, he held her out, saying, "Kiss mommy. Give mommy a kiss." The dog licked my face and he kissed the top of her little black head. The kids were fogging up the window in the dining room trying to see what we were doing.

"Let's go tuck them in," I suggested.

"Come on," He said to the dog, "let's put the kids to bed."

Early the next morning, Kimberly surprised me with an invitation to walk on the bike trail as soon as the kids were out the door. I was lacing up my shoes and pulling my hair back, before we even agreed upon a time to meet. On the trail, the sun teased from behind various thick, white clouds, and it went from blindingly bright to completely dim. We were breathing heavily from our first exposure to physical activity after a long winter, and I couldn't tell if Kimberly was deep in thought or struggling for oxygen. Looking out ahead to the distance before us, I thought of the spiritual journey I had taken. I cleared my throat, confessing, "I raised my kids exactly the way I was raised."

"Humm," Kimberly taunted, looking down at the clock on her cell phone, "You raised your kids already? When?"

I smiled, recognizing the inference of it not being too late, but continued, "Before we moved here, I color coded their clothes and freaked out about the house. I made them be quiet and taught them not to expect too much. Plus, they saw me fading away." I thought about the message they had probably internalized and how they had already been infected with the apple Tony and I had fed them.

As we walked, I felt the separation from my old life, knowing people had grown used to me the way I was. I remembered Kimberly saying, "They come to the cut-out expecting you to poke your head through." Things were so different, I had changed; Tony and the kids were changing too. Like an abandoned house, when someone approached those past images of me, they would wait, but I would not be there. I warned, "People aren't going to know what to think of me."

The trail grew dark when the sunlight was momentarily

obscured by another cloud, but before I could remove my sunglasses, it was bright again. Kimberly smiled at me and acknowledged, "The girl who put on big shows for everyone is gone, huh? You aren't the same person, at all."

"No. I'm not," I answered, feeling relief. But the other side of the mountain offered a panoramic view of the life I let slip away. While I was numb and tired and hiding, time passed. I lost the privilege of living those moments. With my life unfolding in front of me, instead of living and enjoying it, I curled into a ball trying to roll through it as quickly and easily as possible. It hurt to wake up. It cost something to grapple with the emotions of unfathomable joy for seeing the light and the life still before me, and the sorrow from seeing the darkness and life left behind.

Kimberly

I arrived home after our walk marinated in the inescapable truth of the timeline of my life. It had been impossible to accomplish anything as it seemed my mind and soul were cleansing and purging and renewing constantly. Sometimes taking a drive helped me through the detox process. Mentally sifting through memories, I found myself in the neighborhood of the first home Ed and I bought as a married couple. Even though it was just a short drive away, it was a different world from the custom built homes of Westbury.

I drove down the familiar street avoiding the pot holes and cracks still there waiting to be repaired. As I neared my old address, I saw a "for sale" sign in the front yard. *Ed and I spent our first six married years in this place,* I thought. Ed poured his heart and soul into our little, three bedroom, one bath ranch, making it a nice home. We brought three of our four babies home from the hospital to that house.

It had memories.

I painted the rooms in the fun themes of Santa Fe in the kitchen and Mermaid in the girls' room. Ed finished the basement by himself and added a salt water aquarium into the wall. He constructed the tank's pumps using tubes from the hardware store and big, white buckets; it was an engineering feat. I could still see him with his tool belt on coming up into the kitchen after hours of pounding and sawing, to find me irritated with how long he was taking because I wanted a break from the children.

I sat across the street and looked at it for awhile, the way one sits at a loved one's gravesite. You take in the serenity, mourning the missed opportunities, while feeling grateful for the love. I just had to call the realtor to see how she would describe my former life to me on the phone.

In a friendly saleswoman voice, she said, "It's a great starter home. Very cute. The rooms are well proportioned and off the kitchen there is a sliding door to the back yard."

Without warning, I felt myself start to softly cry. Hoping she could not hear me through the phone, I remembered Ed putting in that sliding door and how our home had a plastic sheet covering the opening for a few nights. She continued, "But the best part of the house is the partially finished basement. Well designed, with a beautiful fish tank, built into the wall; very nice." I caught my breath through her long pause, and then she asked, "Have you done a drive by?"

I answered through my tears that I had and hung up. Staring at the house that meant so much to me, I couldn't drive away. I knew the woman once inside was in torment. I sobbed uncontrollably as the last drops of my former life fell into my lap, my eyes fixed on the front picture window looking for the ethereal silhouette of a new mom pacing the green, shag carpet in frustration.

Ed and I were hurting and gauzing all over each other in that house, having no idea how to stop the pain. We were lost and both looking for the other to fix or complete our emptiness within. I thought of the gift of that beautiful family room, and how I stood in it screaming I no longer wanted to be his wife before taking off my rings and throwing them at him. Ed was shouting insults at me, in return. It was Christmas Eve, and we had two beautiful baby girls sleeping upstairs.

I wanted to go back in time and knock on the door to save the couple inside. I wanted to tell the woman what I'd learned. I wanted her to wake up. But I couldn't go back, couldn't save her. I had to live with knowing that time was lost. The time we could have been appreciating one another was wasted on the need. I had to live knowing I'd hurt people with my attempts to stop my pain, thinking I was right. I had to live knowing I did not love my husband, children, friends, or family with purity. I had to live knowing I let myself go because I felt I didn't deserve anything for my own and how I stood there while others hurt me. I unconsciously expected Ed to fix in me what I needed to fix in myself. I was sorry for the weight of my neediness on him and my anger when he didn't measure up. *Only perfect love can complete,* I thought, *only perfect love from God.*

Driving home I switched on the radio and heard Bette Midler singing,

> "It's the one who won't be taken, who cannot seem to give. And the soul afraid of dying, that never learns to live…And you think that love is only for

the lucky and the strong. Just remember that in the winter, far beneath the bitter snow, lies the seed that with the sun's love in the spring becomes the rose."

I sang out the words, and the sound of my voice bellowing through the car made me laugh; I hadn't laughed alone for a long time. It felt good.

The laughter brought with it a recollection of my father at a recent party. He always had a loud, full bodied laugh, which grabs the attention of whoever is near by. Although, at the time I was sitting in another room, it stopped me and I listened to the sounds. It was like putting my ear to a seashell and hearing my soul flow back. *His laugh is a gift*, I thought. I had heard it my whole life. It was a little proof that God loves us so much through the hurts and pains He brings us laughter as endowment, a way to momentarily forget our sorrow. I understood through laugher we could realize hope exists. *It's a reminder that He wants us to live,* I told myself.

Chapter 19

Embracing:
Experiencing Common Ground

Kimberly

I'd become accustomed to the warm sunshine flooding through my bedroom windows each morning on the east side of our home, so my room was a favorite spot. Hearing the pounds of another person's dream being constructed just around the corner, I wondered if their life would change dramatically by living in Westbury just as mine had. Peering out from the shower, Ed asked, "You getting the kids up, or should I?" He was apparently all too aware of my distaste of mornings.

"I got 'em," I smiled pulling on a pair of comfort clothes. Our home was a bit cool, but the sun shined warm on the carpeted spaces under each passing window. I looked at my sleeping son first and then my daughters; they were much smaller a year ago. So much had changed. I was blessed that they loved me through this journey. Ed and I had come through, too. We were communicating on a deeper level and understanding how to best love the other. It was a fantastic spiritual year.

Emerging from the transformation was exciting. Everything seemed new again. I had a feeling of pure joy back in my life, a joy that came from knowing nothing really mattered because I was loved, and yet, by being so loved, everything mattered. I laughed talking to Andrea on our morning call, "Dorothy, you're not in Kansas anymore." I could hear her smiling through the phone. The world was bright with color. Long years of baggage and emotions and pains were gone, completely removed from my mind. I could see clearer than I ever had in my entire life, and the picture was of love. It was of more love than I thought existed, more than I imagined I needed. It was a cleansing and lifting and bliss. It was spring again, this time in my soul.

I began to remember all the great things I'd long forgotten. I used to say I had a terrible memory, but it was all there, walled up behind the shell of a sleepy person, lost and broken. Once the wall was destroyed, I could see again. The speech that I gave in church, which was so rewarding to me when I was only in elementary school, one of my favorite dance routines from sixth grade to the song "City Lights" came rushing back, and the smell and taste of my grandfathers 1914 butterscotch candy was everywhere. We would make it together when I was very small. I remembered how he checked to see if the boiling caramel was thick enough by dropping a tiny spoonful into a cup of cold water and rolling it into a soft ball. It was ready if he could make that ball.

I even remembered my Sunday school teacher, Mrs. James, who I had for years as a child at the Presbyterian Church. She was a retired elementary school teacher and she took things seriously. Wearing the same white dress with big red polka dots and tea colored stains under her arms, she would run around the room shouting, "...and then the great waters split in half!" She had a chart on the wall full of stars and graphs. I remembered the proud look on her face as I placed the blue star next my name for having memorized the books of the *Bible*. I did still know them by heart, thanks to Mrs. James.

I looked at myself in the mirror and could recognize the reflection. Even with the gray hairs trying to poke through, the wrinkles, and the extra weight of 25 years, I could see me. For so long, I did not recognize the woman starring back, as if my reflection made no connection to who I was. How odd it was to be aware of myself again after so many years. "Andrea," I said in exhilaration and tears, "I saw my reflection and knew it was me!" She understood exactly.

Andrea

Being free was exciting. I loved thinking God was glad about me, and it felt so good to experience my feelings. The night of Ed's fortieth birthday, he and Kimberly hosted a huge party in their backyard. They invited the entire neighborhood. We danced and sang and even jumped on the trampoline, laughing and living thunderously. I wasn't advocating for a wild life style, I was simply enjoying myself. Although completely sober the entire time, I drank a bottle of beer with my friends as we danced in the light drizzle to whatever songs the junior high school girls requested. Kimberly and I had incredible fun dancing in the rain, our hair soaked, makeup washed off. I knew life was about more than having fun, but for so long, I didn't even feel alive.

Dancing at the party, I was experiencing the freedom of a child. I enjoyed every moment, and it wasn't until I was dressing to go out a few mornings later that I thought of some Christian neighbors who had been there at the party too. I had no idea if they thought I was a bad witness, or if they thought I was fun or silly. I didn't care. Being a good witness was more important to me than ever, but I came to believe being a good witness meant giving testimony of the One who gave me freedom to be who *I* was created to be.

A critic may wonder if I thought I was created to dance like an adolescent at a back yard birthday celebration. I would only be able to answer, I was created to be unique, a one of a kind light who expresses herself unlike anyone else. Like a snowflake, there was only one of me. From the beginning of time to the end, the only one who could live my life the way God intended was me.

I felt determined to live within the parameters of the law of love, treating other people the way I wanted to be treated and putting God first, but I would never again allow myself to be inordinately concerned with what other people thought of me. The image for approval and acceptance was no longer needed because I knew I was worthy of an opinion and worthy of likes and dislikes. I was free from the anger of being used and from the guilt of hurting other people; I was free from want.

Throughout the year, I had written down much of what we'd discussed. When typed into the computer and saved, there were about thirty pages. I asked Kimberly to try to write her thoughts down too. I was surprised to learn she had already written as much I did. Within minutes, she walked in with her lap top, and we exchanged notes. I told her, "I'm writing this down to send to my brother, Richard… I need your help." Admitting my plan to find the best way of communicating what we had learned, I worried about what he might think of me when he read it. Recognizing the fear behind my feelings, I banished it by embracing the hopes of someday, knowing him for real. Kimberly panned over my collection of thoughts comparing them with her own.

She had the look I'd grown to know as brewing as her eyes shot back and forth across the two computer screens. Keeping her gaze focused on the notes, she suggested, "This is a book. I mean, we have the outline of a book here."

Laughing, I squinted, "Are you serious?" Expecting her to laugh with me, I waited, but she didn't. Instead, she scrolled through the pages on the computer screens in front of us never knowing I had always wanted to write. My house was filled with scraps of paper and notebooks loaded with my thoughts and feelings. I had taken English in college in hopes of teaching literature before I dropped out. My immediate urge was to self-deprecate, listing my inadequacies, but I knew better now. I let her suggestion hang in the room while silently reminding myself I was created and loved and worthy of at least *wanting* to write a book.

Our personal histories were so vastly different yet identical in where we found ourselves. I imagined reading a soul baring disclosure of two women journeying toward truth, and I thought how I had prayed for a relatable roadmap to lead me beyond the valley. We had unearthed the lie of our lives over coffee and prepackaged biscuits. *If we could communicate our process*, I thought, *maybe someone who is struggling could follow it and find freedom too.*

Kimberly

I looked up at Andrea who was deep in thought, and asked her, "Do you remember when we first met and you showed me your *Bible* room?"

"Yes," she answered with a grin.

Clicking my laptop shut, I said, "I noticed something else that night walking into the sitting area off your master bedroom: I saw your journal on the nightstand and a bookshelf full of other journals and works of great literature. It was not hard to notice that you loved books and loved to write." Sitting back in my chair I could see Andrea was the one brewing. Watching her nod in agreement, I quietly assured her, "We need to take these thoughts and keep going, bringing them together periodically as we go."

With that, a new reason to have coffee was born. The book became our regular topic of conversation each day. We wanted to pass it on.

Andrea

Old North Church had since ended their series on L.I.F.E. love, instruction, fellowship, and evangelism. Kimberly and I agreed we'd come full circle in the course of the year. We once only wanted to have fellowship but found love and instruction through hours of coffee and debates. With our book in process, it was our boldest attempt at "E-ing." It was a profound moment considering where our time investment had taken us.

The music that Sunday at church seemed magnificent. If I would have hand-selected the singer and songs myself it couldn't have been more to my liking, but worship had become more about celebrating God than enjoying the service. Nevertheless, it took every ounce of my strength to stay in front of my seat. Crying, I prayed, "It's so good to be me again." I was thanking Him for meeting me in worship. Mr. Clean was just a few rows ahead, praising his heart out as usual; I wanted to yell to him that I knew what he knew. I wanted to tell the whole building full of people I was free. I had traded equity, and I was living in a world where I had everything I needed because I was loved. *I am healed and whole and filled with joy.*

In the following weeks, I experienced an abandon that felt like breathing in crisp spring air after a long winter. Being alive and awake gave me an exuberance I'd forgotten existed. I was seeing Tony the way I should have before we loaded twelve years of life onto our backs and looking at my kids through the eyes of joy, no longer overly concerned with little things.

Kimberly

Once I felt the love of God in my heart and mind, no one had to explain how to love, find compassion, forgive, or accept. No one had to tell me how to stop the anger, let go of revenge, or forget the transgressions of others. I understood for the first time, really understood, how to love one another as a way of living. The emotions were very difficult to put into plain words. The sins, resentments, even unforgivess kept my heart strained back like a hard rock against a sling shot. The tensions of life, my marriage, my career seeming to pull me back tighter and tighter. There were times I almost snapped from the strain. I realized through this awakening that it was *me* holding back the band, struggling to keep it all in control. With God's love, I found the strength to let go. Once released, I soared out into the world unabated. It was profound and beautiful and a little corny, but I would not have traded the feeling for anything in the world.

Christianity and religion were words not intended to evoke others into rule setting, judgmental, and fear-based people. I thought being Christian meant less fun, less love, less truth, and even more boring than the life I lived. What I'd found was the opposite. There was more love than I ever knew existed, more laugh-out-loud fun watching humanity than I realized, and it was so exciting to wake up refreshed and new wondering what the day would bring, watching a dynamic and powerful God unfold the world.

Andrea

Pulling into Westbury Park, I was listening to the car radio with my kids. We heard one of our favorite songs by the Goo Goo Dolls. The poetry of it made me smile and thank God for the day Kimberly asked me to be a true friend and for helping us preserve that authenticity. I sang with them, "I wasn't all the things I tried to make believe I was…" and I knew it was so true for me. I loved the thought of raising my kids to know they didn't have to be who anyone expected them to be. They were born to be free. Parking in the garage, I told myself, *They will grow up learning other people don't have to be who they expect, either. We are so blessed.*

It had been raining for days, but instead of going in, I walked out onto the driveway. Tony opened the door from the house asking what I was doing in the rain. I smiled and rounded the bend out of sight to the front of the house. He came gingerly tiptoeing out through the garage in his bare feet, wanting to know, "What are you doing?"

"I just feel like being out here," I admitted.

He accused me of turning him into a hippie after I kicked off my shoes, too. He'd gone from a man terrified a shred of mulch would soil the side walk to rolling up his dress pants splashing along the gutters barefoot with me. We stomped in the puddles to the pond down the street, looking to see how full it was. I knew the rain would come in our lives as sorrow always does, but it was good news to know we didn't have to wait for paradise.

We had become the family whose house everyone came to for extended family get-to-gethers. Regularly inviting our friends and neighbors into our lives, and viewing those visits as blessings, Tony and I were completely different people from whom we had been a year earlier. Looking at my husband, soaking wet in his work clothes, I thought, *I can love him for who he is, but I will only hold my light up to God, never again to another. My internal flame is for the One who ignited it within me.* I was convinced that nothing, not death, life, angels nor demons, nothing in my past, present nor the future, nothing in all creation would be able to separate me from the love of God that I'd found in Jesus.

Kimberly

For years, I became adept at existing in the darkness while displaying my "angel" to the world, but in these insightful months, the darkness became the place where I would change. So many times, I wanted to run back into the warmth of the sleepy place, but in the comfort, I was not alive. Silence breeds shame, and shame was at odds with a soul wanting more. Emerging from the darkness... letting go of it was the hardest thing I'd ever done, but I found freedom. I could have accepted that my life would never be better, my relationships never stronger, my love stagnant. I could have accepted a life of fears and anxieties wondering how I could control things to make myself feel better, and worried incessantly about "what if." I could have kept my feet planted in discontent becoming madder and madder at the world, depressed at my reflection in the mirror, until I was someone incapable of goodness or love. I could have chosen to fade into self pity or victimization hoping others around me would change and grant me a good life. I could have pretended forever. But I believed in God instead. I believed He meant it when He said He wanted me to live fully and abundantly. I trusted He had a purpose when He created me and it had nothing to do with a lacking soul. I believed in love.

I was so grateful to have the next 37 years to see the world without pretense, to witness the miraculous love of God in the trees, the wind, the sounds of my children, my mother's eyes. I never expected a lifetime of roses and fine wine, or even cheap wine. I understood my experience on this Earth came with hurt, sorrow, and grief. But I am also keenly aware of the presence of God in my life. None of my wounds were as deep, or would they ever be as deep as they could have been without Him.

If I'd learned anything, it was to trust God and the extraordinary love He has for me. That love through Jesus' death, gave me a chance at life, His gift of grace. Accepting that love for others and for myself, I could set out boldly, with my head held strong and high as His child, to live a full life unencumbered and renewed.

Andrea

As Kimberly scooted into the church pew, I asked her, "Did you read the bulletin?" It was the first Sunday I beat her to our regular row.

"No, why?" she asked, reaching for Ed's bulletin.

"They are opening a coffee shop in the new adult education wing here at church. There is a contest to pick the name," I said, knowing she would be thinking the same thing I was.

After the service, Ed urged us both, "Go submit *Common Grounds*. It's a great name for a coffee shop."

Kimberly gestured, indicating she didn't know what to do.

I looked at her reminding, "Well, we really did want to have a café called Common Grounds." Just saying those words, I felt surprisingly excited at the idea of the church's coffee shop and book store.

Walking in to the space of unfinished walls and countertops, we could see the fish bowl of names from across the room. It was full of suggestions, and I felt a bit silly searching my purse for a pen. Kimberly wrote down our submission and tossed the folded paper into the final batch of hopefuls.

She giggled out a whisper, "How many times can we vote?"

Kimberly

A few days passed and I was putting away some storage boxes of winter clothes in the attic. I heard the phone ring and hoped someone was near by. "Are you going to get the phone?" I yelled from upstairs to my family who were busy watching TV. On the fifth ring, I guessed not and answered it myself scooting a box across the dusty floor. I saw it was Andrea. "Hello?"

"Did you get it...get your mail?" Andrea was talking fast and smiling through the phone again. I didn't reply so she just blurted, "We won! Old North is going to name the new café *Common Grounds!*"

We started screaming and I ran to the mailbox for my card and gift certificate, the prize for winning. Ed came running after me down the driveway as I explained they'd chosen our name. We were so excited, I told Andrea that Ed and I would stop by later and bring the champagne. It really felt like a cause for celebration, as if we needed a reason.

That evening in Andrea's kitchen, holding up my champagne glass, I toasted, "To finding common ground."

Clinking her glass with mine, she grinned, "And to the truth that brought an agnostic liberal to her knees and a conservative Christian to her senses."

Andrea

The next Sunday, we definitely got there a bit early. It was fantastic. I'd always wanted a coffee shop named *Common Grounds*, and there it was, constructed beautifully in dark cherry woods and glossy marble. We took a slow walk around the room admiring the hand carved moldings and arched windows. The space looked like the perfect spot to meet a friend, a place to find universal truth and discover the reason to love the people around us. Tony and Ed were happy too. They knew what Old North meant to us, and they knew what finding common ground meant to us as well.

Standing under the domed ceiling, Kimberly handed me a cup of hazelnut coffee. She leaned in until her shoulder bumped mine and suggested, "Let's open the book with a letter to the reader. We should let them know what we hope they find in our story." She was bubbling with excitement, "It could go something like this," closing her eyes, she settled her thoughts and started:

Dear Reader,

If handed a treasure map to the lost world of happiness and peace, where the light within you glowed brightly and drew others; would you accept the challenge? Tracing your finger along the lines of a path not often traveled, would you hazard the journey? Staying asleep, pouring yourself deeper into your work, or hiding yourself away may tempt; as we know. But if you could live the result of your quest, if you were guaranteed to see the world differently from the summit of your soul, would you?

This is a voyage to the center of your heart, taking you back, and then moving you beyond -- to where you are filled to capacity; overflowing into others. The trip will reveal the truth about who you are and how to change, how to let go and how to live fully. We know you desire a full life, not a life filled with material possessions, your image, or your indulgences but of greater bounty than imagined.. an existence where past hurts, bitterness, anger, and fear can be reframed and healed to allow for richness and goodness. A bold life. Your life as it was meant to be lived.

Our prayer is for you to find Him, doing whatever it takes. Scratch, claw up a mud hill, run in the rain of the night, cry, scream, pray silently, but find Him; find the complete and whole message of God. We hope you don't settle for the god of a church; He's not there, nor is He found through the eyes of a priest or pastor. He's neither in a book justifying His existence nor in this book glorifying His name. We found Him slowly, with the love of a friend, and we share with you our struggles to understand and live His life changing message. We invite you to join us in uncovering the apple you were fed.

In gratitude,

Kim & An

Contact Us

We Want to Hear From You!

We want to hear your opinions, thoughts, feelings, and stories. Log on to www.theappleyouwerefed.com to join us in the virtual café... discover the depth of the apple concept and continue unearthing the lie of your life.

While there:

- Download a free workbook to assist you in applying the apple concept.
- Take a quiz to help determine more about your automatic responses.
- Share your experience using apple terms and maybe be among the testimonies selected for our forthcoming new book.
- Find more information about the authors, speaking engagements, upcoming projects, and other valuable resources.
- Link to our favorite internet spots.
- Communicate via e-mail: theappleyouwerefed@gmail.com

We can't wait to hear from you,

Kimberly and Andrea

Acknowledgements

Kimberly

To Ed, I want you to know how much your love and support has meant to me this past year and a half; writing this book, exposing our lives, listening to my thoughts before they were ever written out...thank you for your patience and endurance. Somehow you knew when to leave me alone, and when to carry me away. I love you for so many reasons and now I have one more. (By the way, you are the best dance partner I have ever had...the lessons were such a fun escape.) To Katelyn, thanks for stepping in when I stepped out-locked in my bedroom for far too many hours to be considered legal for a parent. Your responsibility and generous love will always warm my heart. I wish for you the gift of God's limitless love. Let Him nourish you, your whole life. I love you. To Kennedy, thanks for the late night hugs when you somehow knew I needed one. We are both night owls, and I loved your simple gestures of love. I wish for you God's security and comfort.

May He walk beside you on *your* journey, always knowing He has you wrapped with His love. I love you. To David, thanks for the peanut butter and jelly sandwiches with no crust and for not complaining when you didn't get to eat meat for dinner. I loved my daily surprise of your "catch of the day." The big, fat toad will always hold a special place in my heart. I wish for you the pure joy of knowing God's fullness. May you always be aware of the wonderful bounty of a life with God. I love you. To Karaline, thank you for being my personal stylist. You know how to pick out an outfit for mommy, no doubt about that, and I, too, love the pink shimmer lip gloss the best. Your sweet, gentle body curled up to me cat-like as I typed away on the keyboard gave me a reason to keep going. I wish for you to always feel the peaceful love of God. May that tranquility and security surround you throughout your life. I love you. To my sister, Lori. Thanks for the first rough draft edit and encouraging remarks. You endured some difficult phone calls, but sometimes, this girl just needs her sister...I love you. You have a gentle and gracious spirit and I hope you live knowing that despite a sometimes chaotic and crazy world, where people hurt and cause hurt, God's presence brings you peace and serenity. To my brother, Tom. I thank you for talking with me through some crazy conversations. Even though I was nuts...you didn't care and showed me compassion anyway. I love you. You're even temperament is solid and grounded beautifully into life. I hope you feel with God... it is possible to soar. To Sam and Shannon, my brother and sister-in-law, and to Julia, Isabella, Emily, Sammy, and Mia, my nieces and nephew, I want to thank you for all the fun diversions from writing and your love. I love you all very much. To my mother-in-law, thanks for the many "Grandma Jean" days and for sharing your beautiful son with me. I love you. Last, but not least of my family, to my parents, Tom and Janice Semple. I can't thank you. I don't know how, really. I can only thank God for you. I was eternally blessed by you both, in a way that continues to this day. You have always stood beside me as I walked my twisted path, never wavering in your support, including now with this book. Your pure love for me, like God's, is unmerited favor of which I cannot repay. I can only hope to live a life that shows you both how special I think you are, love you back unendingly, and carry forth your generous goodness into the life of my children as a legacy of love inherited from the gift of yours. I love you. A personal thank you to my professor in graduate school, Dr. Dunnerstick. Your philosophy class and kind words about my papers inspired me to continue writing and actually have the nerve to let you read it. Sometimes, people don't realize the impact their generosity has on others, but I hope you do. Thanks for giving me encouragement and telling me I could do it. Finally, to Andrea I thank you for the gift of real friendship. For honest, straight-forward, sometimes ugly, always valued, esoteric yet relatable, butter on the biscuits, sing out of tune, laugh until we snort friendship. Flying is fun with a co-pilot. I have to mention that having you as a part of my life has helped me to change it and live life the way it was intended. I have to mention that God is good, because He gave me the gift of knowing you.

Andrea

Thank you to my whole family for being more important to me than I could ever express on a page in this book. I am especially grateful to all of you for your kind understanding and willingness to be exposed, as I share some of our most personal experiences. I love you, and while I could never possibly show you how much, someday you'll know. Tony, your support, encouragement, and willingness to adapt made this intimidating process so much easier. I love you for a million reasons that make you -- you. If I lived my life a thousand times over I'd find you every time. Ellie, Isaiah, and Tirzah, your level of independence astonishes me. The way you accepted my time investment demonstrated so much love. Sharing my world with you is a joy; it makes life seem too good to be true. Mom and dad, being part of the original six is more valuable to me now than ever. I hope my life communicates the respect, love, and gratitude I have for you. Amy, thank you for the countless hours of conversation and for a lifetime of inseparable friendship. Your honesty proved to be incredibly helpful. Richard, thank you for inspiring me in an unexpected way. Nate, thank you for everything. Kim, thank you for giving me a chance...

Together

Todd and Julie Olson, thank you for opening your lives to us. You were so open and knowledgeable; your patience and willingness to listen and re-explain things has been a special part of our spiritual growth. Much thanks to our small group at Old North Church for the Bible based insight and your willingness to listen as we struggled to learn. Brent and Lori Allen, we appreciate your time investment, effort, and much needed support. Your acceptance and interest speaks volumes to us. We feel blessed to have found Old North Church, where you both continue to give to us and help us grow in ways you will never realize. Special thanks to our editors, without whom this book would have been very different: Shery James, thank you for enduring the first grueling content edit. Your constructive opinions were useful to us as we sought to harness our concept. Nathan Heddleston, thank you for schooling us in the use of the semi-colon and for reminding us that exclamation marks are for children. Your insightful comments were not only invaluable to us, but also hilariously funny. You *are* a genius. To the various local coffee shops and bagel houses, we owe you a great deal of appreciation. You know who you are, but we can't thank you enough for the hours of hazelnut bliss. Finally, to the readers, we thank you for taking the time to read our book. We wrote it mostly for you, and we hope to meet you one day... maybe, for coffee.

Printed in the United States
200768BV00002B/478-564/A